Bygone Industries of the Peak

Julie Bunting

The Peak District Journal of Natural History and Archaeology
Volume 3, 2006

Series editor: Ian D. Rotherham

INDEX

INTRODUCTION

Bygone Industries of the Peak was originally published as a series in the Peak Advertiser, widely recognised for its dedication to historical content. Responses from readers became an important source of additional information, confirming, too, a wide interest in the working lives of those who had gone before. Additionally, through more than 1,000 articles written for the same publication on the most diverse topics imaginable, the writer garnered occasional snippets which would become part of the extended series brought together here.

Writers are constantly vexed by the problem of defining the boundaries of the Peak District. Some publications confine themselves to the Peak National Park, others to the White Peak or Dark Peak, or simply the Peak. Peakland is a personal favourite, borrowed from writers of old, and it has the advantage of providing its inhabitants with their own identity - Peaklanders. For the purposes of this book their domain is treated with some flexibility; in any case industry has a habit of networking.

Similarly, it is not possible to be too pedantic on the question of whether or not these industries are 'bygone' and done with. Cheese making, for instance, continues, as does rope making, albeit 'tied up' with a famous tourist attraction. Some of our old industries live on as handicrafts, but it is doubtful whether today's bobbin-lace maker sees her work as anything more than a pleasure. By contrast, quarrying is still far too active to qualify for this volume, however long its history and importance to the fortunes of the Peak.

Primary sources of research for this work took advantage of living but fast-fading memory, as well as family recollections handed down and never put to paper. Brief stray references in unlikely places were bookmarked over a long period for future use. The files grew fatter, backed by hours of fascinating groundwork, in the literal sense. The Peak is rich in industrial remains, and for the writer their discovery has been the highlight and often the goal of hundreds of walks, as well as the occasional trip underground. It became obvious that there was scope to flesh out specialist research and present the results in individual compact sections.

This is not to underestimate the enormous debt owed to others, from early travel writers like Defoe and Farey to prolific historians such as Dr J.C. Cox and Llewellyn Jewitt, to antiquarians and archaeologists, and groups including the Derbyshire Archaeological Society and the Peak District Mines Historical Society. Special appreciation is due to those individuals who have written about their own special interests, from hat making to water mills, and to village history groups whose publications have provided valuable localised knowledge.

The author would like to acknowledge the assistance of Dr Ian D. Rotherham, at whose suggestion Bygone Industries of the Peak now appear as a single volume, hopefully a worthy complement to the Peak District Journals of Natural History and Archaeology and other titles from Wildtrack Publishing.

Julie Bunting

ABOUT THE AUTHOR

Though Staffordshire born and Nottinghamshire raised, the author considers herself to be an honorary Peaklander, having lived on its borders, vague as they are, for two-thirds of her life. She married a Derbyshire man in one of the Peak's loveliest churches and together they have raised four children who have not yet completely fled the nest. Two small grand-daughters are in line to share in family jaunts, which will no doubt include diversions to look at old lime kilns, mill races, capped mine shafts, packhorse ways, pinfolds, and the like.

Her interests in local history and overseas travel have given Julie Bunting the opportunity to write several books, in addition to features for national magazines and almost 1,200 articles for the Peak Advertiser from its inception in 1982 to date. Her commissions as a freelance television researcher have resulted in occasional appearances in front of the camera and she has made numerous radio broadcasts. In 2001 she moved into a fresh medium as creative writer on the ambitious and highly recommended Peakland Heritage website www.peaklandheritage.org.uk

Work in progress includes a compendium of famous modern day Peaklanders, a subject which, for a change, places the author back in the land of the living.

ALSO BY THE AUTHOR

Fifty Family Jaunts around Derbyshire   J H Hall & Sons 1984

Derbyshire Superlatives   J H Hall & Sons 1985

Fifty Family Jaunts around Nottinghamshire   J H Hall & Sons 1987

Peak Past & Present   Peak Advertiser 1988

Our Peakland Villages   Peak Advertiser 1989

The Peakland Abecedary   J H Hall & Sons 1993

A Peakland Chronology   J H Hall & Sons 1994

Give a Man a Good Name: published in The Seven Blunders of the Peak,

edited by Brian Robinson   Scarthin Books 1994

The Earls & Dukes of Devonshire   Footprint Press 1997

Matlock and Matlock Bath   Tempus 2002

Following The Derwent   Northend 2004

ASHFORD MARBLE

Strictly speaking, Ashford marble is not true marble but an impure form of limestone naturally impregnated with a bitumen. Because it changes from grey to a glossy black when polished, it found popularity as a decorative material. Its existence was even known in prehistoric times, for a dressed slab has been found in a tumulus on Fin Cop above Monsal Dale.

Moving into recorded history, Bess of Hardwick, always loyal to local products, used Ashford marble in 1580 for the chimney-piece of the Great High Presence Chamber at Hardwick Hall - reputedly the most beautiful room in Europe. Just over 100 years later her great-great grandson, the 4th Earl of Devonshire, used it for interior work during his major rebuilding of Chatsworth. In the 1830s, the 6th Duke had massive marble doorways executed at Ashford for the new wing at Chatsworth.

Ashford marble mill was set up on the River Wye in 1748 by Henry Watson. Six years earlier Watson had bought out a marble mason's works at Bakewell, but the mill at nearby Ashford became his main concern. By 1847 the Bakewell mill was operated by John Lomas, who held a lease from the Duke of Rutland on a black marble quarry beside the Bakewell/Monyash road.

Glover refers to marble works at Ashford and Derby, where the material was: "wrought into articles of domestic elegance and into monuments, chimney-pieces are sold at various prices, from 30 shillings to upwards of £60, and beautiful tables of black marble, enriched with elegant engravings, are also made there." Etching and engraving were the only methods used to decorate Ashford marble at that time.

The industry continued to thrive and in 1832 a Mr Oldfield began mining a source in Rookery Plantation on the other side of the river. Demand was set to soar when inlay work was introduced; the glowing floral and geometric designs were an immediate success. Trinkets and jewellery, paperweights and snuff-boxes, crosses, obelisks and barometers were on sale as far as the capital itself. At the Great Exhibition of 1851 the quality and beauty of Ashford marble put even prestigious Italian workmanship in the shade.

Much of the inlay work was carried out in the cottages of Ashford, but workshops were also established in Matlock, Bakewell, Buxton and Castleton - all busy tourist centres with a constant demand for souvenirs. The craft utilised coloured minerals that occurred within easy

1

reach of Ashford. From Nettler Dale in Sheldon came rosewood marble, its reddish bands and white background producing the effect of grained wood when polished. Bird's Eye, a fossil-bearing rock cut to show cross-sections of crinoids, came from Wetton and Sheldon, and a mottled and veined grey marble, varying in tint from faint blue to deep azure-purple, from Monyash. Various shades of barytes were collected from Arbor Low, Bradwell and Castleton, which inevitably also supplied Blue John.

The most prized marble was the rare Duke's Red, found in limited quantities in an unrecorded mine at Alport. The entire supply was extracted and stored at Chatsworth on the orders of the 7th Duke of Devonshire, since which time details of its precise source have been lost. The Dowager Duchess of Devonshire reveals that: "In a dark corner of an underground passage lies a heap of Duke's Red. Andrew [the late Duke] has been known to give a piece of this unique stone to a loved friend." In 1970, Duke's Red marble was incorporated into the Cavendish crest laid near the Great Display House at Chatsworth. More recently, a piece was given to Her Majesty the Queen for the centre of the Garter star in the new Octagon Room at Windsor Castle.

Obliged to mine

The main source of black marble was Arrock Quarry beside the road to Sheldon. This quarry was described by William Adam in *The Gem of the Peak* (1843). Adam was first shown around the marble mill, with its massive wooden machines driven by powerful water wheels, before he was obliged to cross the Wye - "a turbulent stream" - over a plank to reach the quarry. This he described as having: "a bearing of at least forty feet above it of bad measures, as they are called, and the good black consists of nine beds, varying from three to nine inches in thickness ... It is difficult to raise a perfect slab of more than six or seven feet long, and from two to five feet wide. The bearing above the quarry is now so great that they have been obliged to mine it, and support the roofs by the offal stone and strong posts, which makes a visit to it now more interesting."

Blocks of marble were taken across the river to the mill to be sawn to size, ground and polished. By the time Adam's book was published, the plank over the Wye had finally been replaced by a bridge.

Ashford marble remained popular throughout the reign of Queen Victoria; the widowed Queen herself set the vogue for black adornments and jewellery. Turbines were installed at the marble mill towards the end of the 19th century, but tastes were changing and the industry had already peaked. The mill and quarry closed in 1905, although inlay work continued for a few more years until the marble reserves were used up. The site of the works was partly lost in construction of the A6.

Examples of the craft are prized by stately homes, museums and private collectors. Ashford parish church contains a prize-winning table of 1882, reminding the village and its visitors of a time when local skills carried the name of Ashford to all the fashionable cities of Britain.

Water power

BESOM MAKERS

The word besom has passed out of everyday use in little more than a generation and even the written word is at odds with its pronunciation of 'beezum'. Yet the besom has a familiar association in its role as a witch's broomstick! The dictionary definition: 'besom - broom made of twigs tied round stick' adds that the word has been used as a derogatory term for a woman. During research for this article a Matlock man offered the quote: "She's a funny old besom." An updated version may well be "daft as a brush"!

Eighty years ago an elderly Derbyshire man recalled that besom making had been one of the gypsy trades, carried out in quiet country lanes, on commons or out-of-the-way places. He had often come across a gypsy in a lane, busy with a pile of broom or ling (heather) and a dozen or so shafts, making besoms. Over the next few days the gypsy's wife would be seen with an armful or donkey-load of brooms selling them door-to-door.

The method of manufacture involved making a head from a bundle of heather, packed at one end in the centre with smaller twigs to provide a firm bed for the shaft. This end of the bundle was tightly bound with sugar cane, or the more readily available hemp cane, then a tapered shaft was driven and packed into the tightly-bound head. A strong nail was knocked into the cane binding, the business end of the head was trimmed with an axe, and the job was done. A skilled worker could make a besom within five minutes, but a respectable full-time output in a besom workshop was between 60 and 80 a day.

There was a steady demand from housewives who swished their besoms across stone floors, back yards and paths, while farmers sometimes bought a dozen at a time for brushing yards, cleaning out stables, cow sheds and pig styes. Besoms were not used like ordinary brushes but were swung sideways on the half flat. When they got 'clarted up' the dirt was knocked out and the besom left upside-down to dry.

Many villages had a resident besom maker. A former resident of Two Dales, recalling her childhood of the early 1900s, told how she used to visit David Allsop who lived on the hillside above the village. The child enjoyed hitching a lift on Mr Allsop's horse-drawn cart for a ride up onto the moors, where he cut heather to bind into besoms, sold at nine pence each.

In 1851 Stoney Middleton had two families of brush and besom makers, named Jupp and Jackson, who had come from different villages in Sussex. Daniel Jackson was listed as a besom maker at Stoney Middleton in 1895, presumably of Messrs Jackson and Johnson, who carried out this type of work in the chamber over the smithy. Mr E. Jackson was still in business in 1904. In 1901, with one former besom workshop now converted into a cottage, William Jupp's old besom making room was being used for storage by Messrs Cockers, shoemakers. The enclosed yard was still called Besom Shop Yard.

Youlgreave had the fine-sounding Besom Hall, on the left-hand side at the top of steps leading down Bankside. It was described 20 years ago as a derelict cottage with no written record of its past. Hathersage goes one better with a Besom Lane. Besoms were made at outlying Thornhill in part of an old building called The Moot, but this activity died out during the 19th century. It continued somewhat longer at Stone House, described in Sheffield Clarion Ramblers' Handbook of 1930/31 as: "the first house on the left at the top of the hill from Fox House, on the way to Sheffield." At that time a 'broom shop' beside Stone House was in use by William Peat for making besoms, a business which had continued without interruption since started by his grandfather, Henry Peat, in 1826.

Some besom makers were also skilled basket makers. Heather and twigs from East Moor, near Baslow, supported these twin trades at Cutthorpe near Chesterfield, where four particular families were kept in business by demands from the collieries and iron and steel industries of Sheepbridge and Sheffield. Besom and basket making were carried out at Cutthorpe for about 300 years and died out only in the 1960s.

Perhaps besoms are no longer produced in the Peak, but they are still made elsewhere; a time-honoured means of sweeping up dead leaves in the garden, or even as an unused prop in today's 'rustic look' kitchen.

Besom maker

BLEACHWORKS

Bleaching, often in preparation for dying, was an important process in the production of wool, cotton and linen. Before the introduction of chemical bleaching, the strong powers of sunlight did the job simply and cheaply, in much the same way that laundered clothes and linens were kept white by putting them out in the sun, draped over bushes and lawns. On the Upper Tean at Cheadle, where tape was manufactured from the mid-18th century, linen tapes were spread out on open ground for this purpose until the 1930s.

These so-called bleachfields were no match for the vast increases in textile production that came with the Industrial Revolution, and in any case must have seemed distinctly old fashioned. One early advance in bleaching cotton, linen and hemp still saw thread or cloth spread out on grass, but only after it had first been subjected to alternate soaking in an alkaline solution of potash and lime, then washed and soured in buttermilk or bran and water. Unfortunately the whole process was lengthy and expensive.

Change came about with the cheap production of sulphuric acid. It was used to make a liquid bleach for fabrics, even though injurious to health in both manufacture and application. In 1785 the French chemist Berthollet recognised the bleaching properties of chlorine, prompting Charles Tennant of Glasgow to patent a bleaching powder made from a solid compound of chlorine and lime. A process that had formerly taken weeks could now be accomplished within a few hours and give far superior results. Tennant's factory price for the powder in 1800 was £140 per ton; improved techniques meant that 70 years later it cost only £8.50 per ton. The next major means of bleach production was chlorine, often recovered from the waste hydrochloric acid of soda works.

As none of these technological advances was suitable for animal fibres, older bleaching methods continued to be used on wool well into the 19th century. Unspun wool would be de-greased in a solution of stale urine and water, generally in stone troughs known as lants (the name Lant Lane survives at Tansley). This process also lightened the colour of wool sufficiently for dyeing, but for a white finish, largely preferred for flannel, blankets and hose, the wool subsequently had to be stoved or sulphured. Damp wool, whether yarn or fabric, was laid out in a tightly sealed chamber or 'stove' together with containers of burning brimstone. Moisture from the wool was an essential component of the resultant sulphurous vapour, which effected a bleaching process within 12 to 24 hours. Softness was restored by a final wash, sometimes followed by a dip in a very weak solution of indigo dye.

The main problem of this process was that potent condensation tended to drip from the roof and burn holes in the cloth, as did sparks from the brimstone. As time went by, woollen goods faced increasing competition from the cheaper - and whiter - cotton, and stoving began to die out, although the famous Witney blankets continued to be stoved until the 1940s.

A very proper operation

At one time a bleachworks for woollen blankets existed at Brassington, and a Mr Gardom operated a bleaching yard or whitening croft at Bakewell around 1770. It was sited down Combs Road near Spencer Flatt and was supplied with water from Ball Cross and Wicksop springs. Yet the journals of White Watson of Bakewell reveal that in 1816 and 1817 he sent cloth and yarn to, respectively, Mr Tarrand of Tansley and Mr Cawood of Ashover for bleaching.

Trade directories mention William and James Stevenson, yarn bleachers of Wash Green, Wirksworth (1821) and Charles Bower, a bleacher at Nabb House, Darley (1857).

Farey refers to a bleachworks on the Bentley Brook at Lumsdale near Matlock, where evidence of two such undertakings, one with its smithy, survive. A description and photograph of Lumsdale Bleaching Works appears in *The Matlocks and Bakewell*, originally published in 1893. Here the bleaching process began by boiling the cotton in lime and soda, followed by a thorough pummelling with immense steam-driven beaters in soap and water ("A very proper operation", remarked the author, "either for cotton, or little boys and girls even, who have dirty faces"). This vigorous activity was a mere preliminary to further washing, beating and boiling before the goods were transferred to the Patent Vacuum Bleaching Kiers, in which steam-operated air pumps created a vacuum to enable the bleach to penetrate every fibre of the material.

Large quantities of cotton were sent from Manchester to be treated at Lumsdale, although there were closer bleachworks in the northern Peak, as at Fernilee, Chinley, Charlesworth and Glossop. Regular batches also came from Nottingham, Leicester, Loughborough, Coventry and Derby. It was noted in *The Matlocks and Bakewell* that the Lumsdale works had been in the Farnsworth family for 80 years and that, furthermore, they were "well calculated to uphold the prestige that these works have borne for more than 200 years." Trade directories at the turn of the 19th century list two other bleachers at Lumsdale: Edward Garton, and F. H. Drabble of Tansley Wood Mills. Messrs Drabble were also dyers - a side of their business which continued until 1999; their bleachworks, like all others in the Peak, had already been lost to progress.

Dying cloth

BOBBIN MILLS

The production of wooden bobbins was a spin-off from the textile industry. Yarn or thread was wound onto these cylindrical spools, to be unwound in a smooth continuous movement during the weaving process. A large cotton-spinning mill would have several million bobbins in use day and night, giving rise to a constant demand for replacements as they became worn and damaged.

Bobbins were shaped from coppice wood and generally manufactured in a water-powered mill close to the timber source. New wood had to be dried before use, so was stored for a time in drying sheds. In some mills, the turning machinery and lathes produced other cylindrical wooden items such as tool handles and cotton reels. As with bobbins, a smooth finish was essential and production was completed in the polishing section.

A specific type of bobbin, very slender and about 4" (10 cm) long, was used in making pillow or bobbin lace, a speciality of the Middleton by Youlgreave area in the 18th/19th centuries. Middleton had a bobbin and tape mill built in 1822 on the River Bradford, on the left-hand side of the lane leading up into the village. (see Tapes and Narrow Fabrics) A dam supplied power via a large overshot water wheel. The mill was unoccupied by 1846, but the water wheel later helped to raise the village's piped water system.

Lace bobbins were commonly made from fruit tree wood or bone, weighted at one end with a circle of beads threaded onto wire. Many bobbins were in use on each piece of work and the addition of flat-sided beads stopped them rolling about on the supporting pillow. A bobbin-net machine for lace making was invented around 1803. (see Lace Making) Authentic pillow lace bobbins are popular with antique collectors and reproductions are also available.

Manufacture of larger commercial bobbins was often carried out in close proximity to major customers, as on the western outskirts of the Peak, where textile mills at Mellor supported a number of bobbin turners throughout the 19th century. Twelve were listed in the 1850 census, one of whom, Jesse Stafford, was still in business 20 years later, employing eight men and five boys.

Around 1795 a venture known as Wightman's bobbin factory was established at Fritchley, but the original building burnt out in 1885 - a dam and mill tail mark the site. A bobbin mill was recorded at Lumsdale near Matlock in the early 19th century, possibly that owned by Edward Radford, and run in conjunction with a large spinning and candlewick mill nearby. At Bradwell, the Fox family manufactured weavers' shuttles for the numerous cottage looms in the locality.

Reconstruction

There is scant evidence to support a local tradition that bobbins formed the early output of Ashford Mill in Ashford Dale. There may have been some confusion with a saw and wood-turning mill built at Lumford, Bakewell in the 1870s and operated by the Frost family.

The Arkwright Society is currently refurbishing Slinter Cottage, a small mill on Bonsall Brook in the Via Gellia. It is thought to have been built between 1800 and 1830, probably as a slag mill, and retains its water wheel. The subsequent installation of wood-turning machinery and evidence of coppicing in the area suggests bobbin production - the building is only a short distance from the famous Cromford cotton mills. In its later working life, the little mill on the brook certainly functioned as a wood-turning and sawmill, with domestic accommodation on the upper floor.

Prior to its purchase by the Arkwright Society in 1991, Slinter Cottage had been maintained and preserved for 50 years by its lady owner. Put up for sale at £65,000, its historical significance attracted a contribution of £55,000 from the National Heritage Memorial Fund. Further financial assistance came from the Zochonis Trust and the Alan Evans Memorial Trust.

BONE MILLING AND DUNG PROCESSING

Memories are fading of the once regular rounds of the rag-and-bone men, and the younger generation may ask why anyone would want to buy tatty rags and smelly bones. The answer is that the former were recycled for paper making and the latter for glue, gelatine, fertiliser and pottery manufacture. In 1799 Josiah Spode founded the Minton works at Stoke on Trent, using bone ash for his 'natural soft paste' porcelain - i.e. bone china.

Animal bones have been used for land improvement for hundreds of years and demand grew alongside the agricultural revolution. Bones, and the bony cores of ox-horn, were crushed at water powered grinding mills between iron wheels or rollers. The bones were sometimes first boiled in cauldrons to extract the grease, otherwise bone manure was very attractive to vermin, birds and insects.

Farey refers to bones also being pounded under forge hammers, which connects with the story of Strutts of Belper asking their workpeople and their families to save bones, paying them 1s.6d. (7.5p) per hundredweight and taking wheelbarrows full at a time. Strutts had the bones broken up at their Makeney forge for spreading on their own pasture land.

Tanyards were a good source of bone and horn. More unusually, Sheffield knife-handle makers sold their horn trimmings direct to local farmers, as did horn and bone button manufacturers. Farey notes that: "Several ship loads of the bones, collected in London (some from the churchyards as I have heard) find their way to the interior of Derbyshire annually and are there ground by mills." He lists nine bone mills in the county, including one at Ashford with iron water wheels powered by the Wye, and one described as 'the slag mill rollers' in the Via Gellia, Bonsall Dale. The Ashford mill later became a sawmill and that in Bonsall Dale was taken over by Cromford Garnetters.

Mills commonly adapted to changing times and new uses. Longnor corn mill on the Manifold was enlarged post-1831 to allow for bone crushing. This activity continued until 1890, although corn milling had ended 20 years earlier. A lead-smelting mill at Lumsdale, near Matlock was replaced by a bone mill. Worked from a millpond fed by a leat from Bentley Brook, the mill ground calcined or burnt bones for fertiliser and for use in pottery manufacture. A mill on the Mill Brow stream at

Ludworth, originally built to grind corn, is believed to have been worked by two men as a bone mill before the building was washed away by a flood in the early 1920s.

In the late 19th/early 20th century, James Frost operated as a bone crusher at Bakewell Field, Sheldon. A slightly later reference connects to a knacker's yard and bone mill between Middleton by Wirksworth and Brassington, on a site eventually developed by Magnesium Elecktron Limited.

A bone and madder grinding mill was established around 1780 at Turf Lee near Marple. Known as Springwater bone mill, it also supplied Strines Printworks with red-madder dye extracted from roots of the madder herb. In July 1833 the premises were advertised to be let, with mention of a two-storey building, a 10h.p. engine and a spring water supply of 40 gallons per minute. The business was put up for sale in 1865. Trading as the Marple Bone-Dust, Glue and Size Company, the operation comprised a nearly new plant on the canal near the Goyt aqueduct, equipped with a disintegrator, bone-dust sieving machine, wooden boiling cisterns and a large number of glue coolers. Glue and size was on sale from the premises 20 years later, trading as Marple Chemical Company. Its proximity to the Peak Forest Canal was presumably a useful asset when subsequently converted to a calico mill.

Soap suds and scavengers

Bone manure was considered particularly good for turnip crops, bettered only - according to Farey's sources - by privy soil, i.e. human waste. The practice of adding small quantities of lime to privies to absorb the stench was observed at Peak Forest. This was considered less satisfactory than adding earth, which produced a drier manure ready for spreading.

Privy soils were combined with 'town dung' to produce an effective manure on fallow land, used with soap suds and 'other produce of the sewers' at Belper. Some towns had a communal dung-hole for dung, weeds, etc. Improved versions were kept well wetted to produce liquid manure, extracted from beneath the pile. Town dung consisted largely of horse and other animal droppings swept off the streets by town scavengers, a recognised trade. It was sold by the cart-load or by weight to local farmers. In 1808 the price at Ashbourne and Matlock Bath was seven shillings (35p) a ton.

Most farmers recycled output from their own livestock, often using 'yard dung' collection points of their own design. On some large farms, soakage from cattle stalls and dung yards was left to drain into storage tanks. Farey describes how Mr Joseph Gould of Pilsbury took care to prevent his dung yards from becoming drenched by rain. It was a simple matter of fixing launders to the outbuildings - not normally a priority, it seems.

The farmyard dung heap is still good farming practice, but other rural methods of fertiliser production have passed into history, taking with them the bone crushers, town scavengers, privy soil collectors, rag-and-bone men and - thankfully - communal dung-holes.

12b Horse-mill with edge
runners. Pyne's Microcosm,
1803.

Horse mill

BOOT AND SHOEMAKERS

This ancient craft was always interdependent on other trades and industries. A time-served cobbler properly belonged to the profession of cordwainers, whose Liveried Company carries the motto 'With Leather and Skill'. A 19th-century Apprenticeship Indenture has been handed down in the family of a young man apprenticed to Thomas Revill in Hathersage, at the rather high cost to the lad's father of 10 shillings (50p) a week. The young man became a hand-sewn boot and shoemaker in Grindleford for over 30 years, then later when hand-sewn shoes became too expensive, he became the village repairer. He was very proud to hold the profession of cordwainer - the word 'cobbler' was never to be mentioned in his presence.

A good pair of boots or shoes made all the difference to everyday comfort, whether in the workplace or not, and they had to last. In poorer families, and not so very long ago, people often had only one pair of shoes to their name. For children that meant hand-me-down boots as often as not.

No one had to go far to buy footwear as a village of any size was likely to have a resident shoemaker. Even the leather was usually local, obtained from the nearest tannery, as at Stoney Middleton, where there seems to have been a commercial connection between bootmakers and Grindleford tannery. (see Tanners and Leather Workers)

In the 1830s Bakewell had up to 40 shoemakers. Tideswell, Winster and Matlock Bath each had seven, Hope three, Bradwell three, Hathersage and Calver each had two. By 1857 Bakewell supported only eight, but more than 20 were in business at Wirksworth, 19 at Matlock, 13 at Ashbourne, seven each at Baslow, Eyam, Winster and Hartington and six at both Bradwell and Bonsall. One-man businesses were found in countless other hamlets and villages.

Out on strike

Footwear production is particularly associated with Eyam and Stoney Middleton. Around 1830 the former had nine boot/shoemakers and the latter six, plus one saddler. What began as a cottage industry grew into thriving family concerns, employing relatives and neighbours working with simple machinery. Production expanded into disused textile factories and purpose-built premises. The majority of workers were women on piecework, though women outworkers at Bradwell and Hathersage took in work from the Eyam factories, machining uppers in their homes. A small number of men carried out heavy cutting work at the factory, originally by hand with a sharp knife. Later on, sole and heel pieces were stamped out by heavy machinery which invariably claimed at least one finger or thumb from every operator - the price of cutting a dozen pieces of leather per minute. Lads as young as 13 spent long, monotonous hours inking boot edges - up to 1,000 pairs a day for four shillings (20p) a week.

Girls and women machined the five or six sections of uppers together, often working by the light of candles that they had to buy for themselves. Women grew round-shouldered and developed poor eyesight, while severe breathing problems affected men involved in the final buffing and scouring of leather and brass rivets, when the air was thick with particles of sand-paper, leather and fine brass.

Yet any job was welcome and by 1910 Eyam and Stoney Middleton shared three wholesale boot, shoe and slipper manufacturers. Stoney Middleton concentrated on producing men's working boots, including army boots during the First World War. There was, however, increasing competition from larger concerns, while subsistence wages and long hours were attracting the attention of the trade union movement. In 1913 local workers were receiving £1 for a 63-hour week, half the national average for the trade. And with only a 15-minute dinner break, the shoemakers of Eyam barely had time to run home, bolt their food and run back to work.

At the risk of immediate dismissal, many employees joined the Boot and Shoe Operatives Union. On taking up the post of secretary of the Eyam Branch in January 1918, Bill Slater was sacked by his employers, Ridgeway Bros. Then bosses played a cruel card in declaring that they would no longer request exemption from call-up for any employee of military age who had joined the union. Employers refused all attempts at negotiation and a strike was called on 28 February 1918 involving seven local footwear firms.

Six months later, by which time £1,566 had been paid out in strike pay at Eyam (out of a national total of £1,589), the dispute was raised in Parliament. Nevertheless, and in spite of some headway at Stoney Middleton, the strike dragged on until 1920 without achieving union objectives. The concluding union report read: "We are relying on a Government Bill to make law a 48 hour week and a minimum rate of wages agreed by the Association of Employers and Workmens Union."

Production resumed, continuing at Stoney Middleton until around 1970, some time after it had ceased at Eyam. (Related items of local origin are on display in Eyam Museum.) Most smaller shoemakers had also bowed to big business. Longnor was typical of Peakland villages where the end came with a falling demand for lead miners' and quarrymen's boots; a necessity that had supported many workshops well into the 20th century.

The Shoemaker

BUTTON MAKERS

Buttons have survived the invention of modern day fastenings, even if they no longer serve any useful purpose on some items of clothing. A suit might have two or three buttons on the cuffs, whilst a tail-coat has two buttons right in the middle of its back. These details are anachronisms from the days when a man regularly travelled on horseback. He would be dressed in a long coat with flying tails, which flapped against the horse's sides and got hairy and greasy. So he had two buttons put on the back of his coat and buttoned up his coat-tails behind him. He also wanted his arms as free as possible, especially when out hunting, so the ends of his sleeves were slit and buttons sewn along the cut. The sleeves could then be doubled back and buttoned down.

Our use of buttons as fastenings goes back no further than the 15th century in England. Buttons were originally merely decorative, but gradually came to replace lacing, especially on clothing such as ladies' bodices. Ivory was the earliest material to be used, whilst brass buttons were being produced by the latter part of the 17th century. Rapid growth in trade came with the Industrial Revolution. Around 1745, Matthew Boulton introduced a number of improvements in button manufacture and in 1767 his son established a works in Soho. He obviously numbered the gentry among his customers, for his top quality steel buttons with facets sold for almost a guinea each. Early buttons did not have holes, but a shank, or loop, enabling them to be sewn to the garment. A method came into use in the early 19th century whereby a filling of cloth or pasteboard was sandwiched between two metal discs which were then clamped together.

Only brief details survive of the manufacture of lead buttons on the top floor of the Manor House at Wetton, accessible to workers from an outside staircase.

Buttons were made in and around Flash on the Staffordshire moorlands well into the 1800s. Small round moulds of wood were dyed in mineral springs and then encased in silk, brocade, etc. to suit their purpose. Covering buttons provided work for many women in their own homes, using skills passed down from mother to daughter. They put in long hours to earn as little as 8d (3.3p) per gross. This intricate work produced web-like designs from single gossamer strands of silk, so fine as to be almost invisible. Button merchants kept the women supplied with thread from the silk mills of Leek and Macclesfield, collecting the finished work for despatch to London, Bristol, Scotland and overseas. Some families seem to have worked independently, their menfolk hawking home-made buttons around the countryside.

Brass buttons were made in Hathersage on the top floors of a row of 3-storey cottages on Besom Lane and, from around 1720, at a mill on Dale Brook. The metal came from Sheffield, to where finished buttons were returned. Manufacture continued at Dale Mill until about 1824 when needle production took over. (see Pins and Needles)

Brass buttons could be mass-produced using stamping machinery, whereas other materials needed individual attention. Pierced buttons allowed a greater choice, as they did not need a shank. Even porcelain was introduced in the mid-1800s, whilst a widely adopted new French process produced a suitable material from cattle hooves, softened by boiling. Horn had been in use since the previous century. Mother-of-pearl buttons enjoyed lasting popularity, made from pearl oyster shell cut into discs, polished and pierced. Oyster shell was imported from the colonies, and London became the centre of the world's trade in mother-of-pearl buttons - and the kingdom of the famous Pearly Kings and Queens.

Nowadays we have press studs, zips and toggles, but buttons are still holding firm ... and whoever heard anyone say: "Oh, he's got all his Velcro sewn on"?

CANDLE MAKERS

Not only do candles have a long history as domestic lighting but, here in the Peak, they had extra importance as an essential to the lead mining industry. So it is not surprising that many mining villages had a chandler's workshop.

Knowledge of candle making developed from the earliest known lamps, which consisted of a fibrous wick of some sort, stuck into grease or oil which rose up the wick as fast as it burned away. The early Phoenicians are thought to have progressed into making solid candles by running a thread of yarn through beeswax. The tallow candle is probably Roman in origin and utilised the harder types of animal fat, although a few species of trees were found to yield vegetable tallow.

Until late medieval times, simple domestic lighting was provided by rushlights, made in the home by soaking the pith of a rush in melted household grease and leaving it to set. Rushlights were the forerunners of tallow dips - basic candles made by dipping a wick into a tank of melted tallow, drawing it out to set, then dipping and cooling again until it was thickened to size. A simple dipping frame allowed several to be made at once. Metal moulds were also used in the home, turning out perhaps half-a-dozen candles at a time, tapered for easy removal. A thread was run through the centre of each hollow cylinder before the melted wax was poured in from the broader end. Once hardened, the candles were simply tapped free.

Beeswax produced excellent candles, but most people knew only the cheaper tallow variety. A combination of mutton and beef fat gave the best quality tallow, plain beef fat was second best and pig fat was cheapest of all, but gave off an unpleasant smoke. In the latter half of the 18th century a new fuel, spermaceti, became readily available. Obtained from the head of the sperm whale, this white waxy substance was also used as a base for ointments. In candle manufacture it was sometimes scented with plant oils, offering a pleasant alternative to smoky and smelly oil lamps.

Castleton inkle

The first commercial moulding machine with a continuous wick was invented in 1834, producing up to 500 candles at a time. Improvements to candlewick came with the introduction of thin plaited braids made from cotton and inkle (flax). Inkle was one of the products turned out by the rope makers of Peak Cavern at Castleton. (see Rope Makers) This was the scene recorded around 1812: "On one side were the young girls belonging to the inkle manufactory, turning their wheels, winding thread, and amusing their companions with cheerful songs." Elsewhere there is mention of 'beggar's inkle' on sale at Ashford around 1820.

Because early wicks were not completely incinerated in the candle flame, the charred tip needed to be frequently snipped off, or 'snuffed'. An important new process was invented in 1825, whereby candlewick was 'pickled' in a chemical solution. This allowed the burning ash to fuse and become completely consumed.

Derbyshire was the source of the world's first paraffin wax candles. In 1847, the brilliant scientist Sir Lyon Playfair identified the presence of petroleum oil in a Riddings coal pit. The discovery led to the establishment of the country's first oil refinery, but the enterprise seemed threatened when the condition of the oil changed. Playfair was consulted and recognised the presence of paraffin in the oil. This he extracted to produce two wax candles, used to illuminate one of his own lectures at the Royal Institution.

Paraffin wax candles came into wide use, often containing stearine as a stiffening agent. Meanwhile, the use of tallow continued for quite some time, especially in mining villages such as Stoney Middleton, Winster - in premises at the top of Woolley's Yard, and Monyash, where a tallow candle factory operated behind the house known as 'Chandlers' on Rakes Road. The proprietors, Messrs Harrison, obtained their tallow from local butchers. And at least two generations of a family named Bobanks made candles near the village green at Tansley. In 1896 their former chandler's shop and the adjoining properties were converted into living accommodation under the name Fir Cottages.

More than a century on and candles are still irreplaceable, popular now for their perfumed, decorative shapes and essential for occasions from birthdays to barbecues.

CHEESE MAKING

Cheese is referred to in the Old Testament, so we can be certain that it has a long history. Greek and Roman warriors ate cheese to give them strength, and in spite of today's move away from fatty foods, there are now more varieties than ever before.

For hundreds of years, cheese making was a particular skill of farmers' wives. Some produced only enough for their own family, but cheese was far easier to sell than surplus milk and brought in useful income to the dairy farmer. Weekly cheese markets took place at Derby, Ashbourne, Bakewell, Chesterfield, Uttoxeter and Leek, with annual cheese fairs held in and around the Peak, including Bakewell, Tideswell and Winster. Along with oatcake, Derbyshire cheese formed the staple diet of both Peakland lead miners and coal miners in neighbouring counties. Great quantities of Derbyshire cheese were always taken to Nottingham Goose Fair.

Cheese making was very strenuous work, though generally left to the farmer's wife, daughter, or dairymaid. On a larger farm the process began with the dairymen bringing milk straight from the milking sheds to be poured into a huge vat. The addition of rennet turned the milk into a solid mass of curd. Until rennet became commercially available as an essence or powder, it had to be obtained more directly. Typically this involved nailing the dried and salted skin of a calf's stomach to the kitchen wall, with a piece of newspaper behind to keep it from marking the paint. A piece of skin would be cut off and left to soak in water overnight. It was this liquid that was poured into the fresh milk.

The resulting curd was thoroughly broken up then lifted out and placed in large sieves lined with muslin, or cheese-cloth as it was called. The corners of the cloth were tied over the curd before it was weighted down and left to drain for a short while. Next it was cut into slices to be worked into fine crumbs with the hands, then salted and tied up again, this time with a metal hoop between cloth and sieve to give the cheese its final shape. Finally, the last drop of whey had to be pressed out. One distinctive method, called 'queedling', involved placing the cheese on a rigid perforated board beneath a queedle - a strong plank several feet long with one end firmly bolted into the wall. The dairymaid, and often a farmhand or two, sat on the loose end of the queedle and moved it up and down like a see-saw, pressing the cheese against the perforated board.

It only remained to place the cheese into a large stone press. Presses had heavy weights attached to their sides and could be further tightened by means of a screw. They often held several cheeses. As a new one was added, the oldest was taken out to be stored in a cool garret or cellar. Every morning the dairymaid had to sweep the stored cheeses with a clean soft brush, turning them over about once a week.

Derbyshire cheese was uncoloured and heavy in texture, with a generally mild flavour. John Byng, having dined at Ashbourne in 1790, wrote: "the cheese of this country pleases me much; being a medium between the Cheshire and the Stilton." In fact Derbyshire cheese was often passed off in London as the more expensive Cheshire. As far back as the late 17th century, London cheesemongers were spending up to £500 on 'Derbyshire and Staffordshire cheeses and butter' at Uttoxeter market in a single day.

Trade gradually came under the influence of cheese factors, whose price-fixing activities alternately incurred the anger of producers and consumers. The food riots of 1766 were partly directed against these middlemen. Matters obviously settled down, for in the 1790s Robert Thornhill of Great Longstone regularly had cheese brought from Longnor by packhorse, possibly to be resold around Longstone but also further afield. A record of 1796 refers to 12 cwt delivered from Bakewell to Longstone and then sent on to Sheffield. Within a seven-day period the following year, Thornhill paid for three tons of cheese to be taken directly to Ashford from Longnor. Between 1814-18 he was also selling cheese to Matthew Furniss of Chesterfield, presumably a retailer. Quite a number of cheese factors were in business around Longnor, Hartington and Sheen in the mid-19th century.

Cheese factories

A 1794 report on Derbyshire farming stated that cheese was: "the chief, if not the only article of provision which the natives can spare out of their own country." The Dove Valley, with its good grazing, was particularly productive dairying country, and it was a member of an old Sheen family who introduced pioneering manufacturing methods to the Peak. William Gilman by name, his speciality was a 40lb Derbyshire cheese. In 1862 he won first overall prize at an international exhibition in London. Gilman studied and demonstrated cheese-making methods in Russia, America and Holland. He maintained a lengthy correspondence with Russian cheese makers, one letter referring to more than 130 cases of Derby cheese sent to Mockba. A Mr Veristchagin wrote: " ... we shall never forget the service you rendered" - and from Anna Muromsoff came: "... the Dairy business is making rapid progress in Russia, my Moscow friends who you know, are now very well-off and living as Lords ... and that our Russian Derby-cheese had the prize in the cheese show."

Gilman is credited with establishing England's first purpose-built cheese factory in 1870 at Longford, near Derby. Others followed and within a few years Derby cheese was being produced by Gilman and others in factories at Hope Dale, Ecton, Reapsmoor, Gratton, Woodeaves, Grangemill, Glutton Bridge and Hartington - where pigs were kept to consume the whey. As an indication of what the industry meant to local farmers, three out of the four farms at Hollinsclough sold their entire milk output to the Glutton Bridge cheese factory.

A good annual average of cheese per cow was around 3 cwt, but cheese was made for only 7/8 months of the year due to the poor quality of winter milk, at least until the advent of improved winter cattle feeds. Between mid-April and mid-November, milk arrived at the factories in anything from buckets slung from shoulder yokes to 30-gallon churns. Factory hands put in long hours and seven-day weeks to keep pace with supplies.

Reapsmoor cheese factory, near Sheen, was run on co-operative lines. A number of farmers contributed labour towards its construction; others bought £5 shares. Originally called the Hulmes Dairy, it changed name and ownership several times. Between 1936 and 1950, as Express Dairies Ltd, the factory produced the original Derby cheese as well as Cheshires, Cheddars and Caerphillys. Right up until its closure the factory was buying milk from over 30 farmers: it continued as a milk depot for a further two years.

Ecton cheese factory stood on the site of an old ore smelter, above an adit connected to abandoned copper workings. Following complaints that factory waste was polluting the River Manifold, a pump was installed to discharge the whey below ground into the Clarion Mine. Explorers who visited the 'Whey Level' in the 1940s came across a "peculiar smell and whitish stickiness underfoot."

During the past century, cheese making in the Peak has almost come to an end. The decline set in as urban growth brought increasing demands for fresh milk. Whereas lack of fast transport had once made it impossible to sell milk any distance from the farm, the railway could deliver supplies into the industrial towns and cities of the North and Midlands. The morning milk train became a way of life for dairy farmers, and was far more profitable than supplying local cheese makers.

Factories gradually closed down until only Hartington was left to keep Peakland cheese on the map. After standing empty between 1894-1900, the factory was taken over by Thomas Nuttall, a Stilton cheese maker from Melton Mowbray. He began producing Stilton at Hartington and the business was later expanded by his son, John M. Nuttall. In the 1920s/30s Hartington cheese was supplied to King George V by Royal Warrant. Hartington Blue Stilton is now world-famous, though the factory produces a range of varieties, bringing 21st-century technology to this age-old skill.

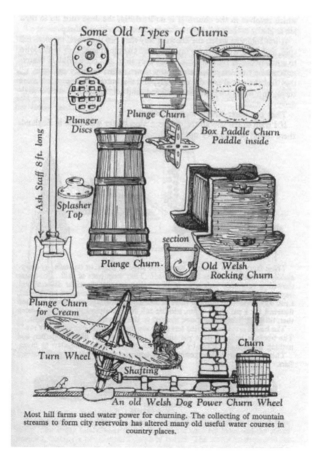

Some Old Types of Churns

Ash Staff 8ft. long

Plunger Discs

Splasher Top

Plunge Churn

Plunge Churn

Box Paddle Churn
Paddle inside

section

Plunge Churn.

Old Welsh Rocking Churn

Plunge Churn for Cream

Turn Wheel

Shafting

Churn

An old Welsh Dog Power Churn Wheel

Most hill farms used water power for churning. The collecting of mountain streams to form city reservoirs has altered many old useful water courses in country places.

CHERT MINING

In geological terms, chert is classified as a mono-minerallic rock, a fine-grained, flinty silica most commonly found in veins in the uppermost beds of the limestone sequence. Chert was worked into tools in prehistoric times, easily shaped by chipping off flakes to produce sharp edges. Scrapers and awls have been found at a Mesolithic site at Stoney Low, Sheldon.

The most useful role for chert was recognised about two centuries ago for the grinding of calcined flint, used as a whitening agent in earthenware manufacture. In 1772 the potter Josiah Wedgwood recommended Derbyshire chert as a major improvement over granite millstones, which left annoying black specks in the pure white flint. In a *Report on Mines and Quarries in Midland District* (1897), Stokes describes how chert was "of special value for china works where the large blocks are used as millstones made to revolve round and upon a floor paved with the smaller blocks grinding away the chertstones."

Blocks of Derbyshire chert were initially taken into Yorkshire and Staffordshire by packhorse or cart, but from 1793 considerable quantities went by road to Cromford Canal for shipment to the Potteries. In due course the stone was despatched by rail.

Chert was also known as hornstone or petrosilex in the Peak. Although black, and black and white chert occurs, the white 'china stone' variety was found in only a few worthwhile deposits. Major extraction took place in Bakewell at Holme Hall and Holme Bank Mines and Pretoria Quarry, and also from pits west of Great Longstone. Smaller mines and quarries existed at Bakewell, Ashford, Masson Hill, Bonsall and Over Haddon pastures.

Pits, quarries & mines

Numerous records concerning the Longstone chert industry are contained in *About a Derbyshire Village* (Wright). A reference of 1784 mentions the sum of 6s 9d paid to Samuel Furniss for "Getting Chert Stone at 1s 6d pr Day." Another entry reads: "Agreed with Saml Ashton & Jos Garrot to get Chert Stone for me upon Scrater at 1s 6d per tun." Costs are shown for gunpowder and for delivery from Longstone chert pits to Chesterfield Wharf, Cheddleton, Gyte Moss, Longnor Bridge and on to Leek. Transport to Cromford and Buxton Moss appears in early 19th-century entries. A trade directory of 1900 names William Millington as a chert merchant at Great Longstone but he is not listed in subsequent directories.

The last two operational chert mines in Derbyshire were the Pretoria Mine and Holme Bank Mine, both at Bakewell. Pretoria opened in 1902. Access was from adits in a quarry at Bank Top and the steep workings extended beneath the road to connect with the earlier Greenfield shaft. The chert bed lies on a 1 in 3.7 gradient and the mine was subject to flooding in severe winters. Illumination was by mains electricity in addition to carbide lamps carried by the miners.

The chert bed was on average 9ft (2.7m) thick, though up to 18ft (5.5m) in places. It was extracted by removing the underlying limestone so that the chert fell under its own weight. A hoist powered by compressed air loaded it onto flat wagons, drawn to the surface by compressed air winches along a 1ft 6in (46cm) gauge railway. The 'waste' limestone was built up into substantial roof supports.

Between the wars the number of employees, which in 1905 totalled 38, fell to about a dozen and by 1964 was reduced to four, only two of whom worked underground. Commercial output from Pretoria ended in 1968/9.

Early 19th-century extraction at Holme Bank was from quarries, but commercial mining was in place by 1867, when the site was known as Bakewell Chert Mine. Later it was also referred to as Smith's Mine, after the owner. The workings consisted of an extensive system of passages with eight entrances.

In 1892, an account of a visit to Holme Hall and Holme Bank mines was published in the *Derbyshire Advertiser*. The owner of Holme Hall, Mr Alsop, had a major problem on site at the time: "The water, which had since the opening been a great preventative to the successful working of the mine, at length gained the mastery and, notwithstanding the employment of heavy and costly machinery, caused the men to retire from the place."

By contrast, Holme Bank Mine, the property of Messrs Smith of Burton-on-Trent, was completely dry throughout. The newspaper reporter was given a lighted candle and taken by a workman to one of the work faces, over a quarter of a mile from the entrance. About 40 men were labouring by candlelight, many engaged in cutting up a 20-ton block of chert recently 'blown down' by gunpowder or dynamite. Broken up into a manageable size, the stone was removed on wheeled trucks drawn on rails by small ponies.

Blocks weighing 100 tons were occasionally blasted free and although the supply was good, the demand was even better, with large orders arriving from Scotland as well as the Staffordshire potteries. Great piles of chert were normally stocked in the yard of Bakewell railway station, but 1892 was such a good year that these were almost used up.

In view of the flourishing state of the industry, the reporter was highly critical of the 17 or 18 shillings (85-90p) a week paid to the hard-working miners. Some had 25 years' experience and all worked long hours underground. "What would a collier think of this?" asked the visitor. "Wouldn't he strike hard and very often until it would be at least doubled?"

In 1925, 41 men were employed, but 20 years later only 21 were at work. Approximately half worked underground. Between the two World Wars, mining broke out on the surface, enabling the chert to be quarried alongside limestone. In its later years the mine met a considerable demand for poultry grit. Holme Bank Chert Mine closed between 1959 and 1961. A block-making plant operated on the site in the 1960s, using existing supplies of chert in the manufacturing process. Extraction had already ended.

Today the few underground visitors to Holme Bank Mine include cave divers who use the pure underground waters for training purposes. Almost 10 years ago the Peak Park Planning Board granted planning permission for the mine to be opened up to visitors but this seems to have been put on hold.

CLOG BLOCK CUTTERS

A stream rising just south of Wirksworth is the infant River Ecclesbourne, the 'eccles' element of its name believed to refer to the nearby parish church. The course of the river was followed by the now disused Wirksworth to Duffield branch of the Midland Railway, giving access to mainline stations as well as bringing passengers into Wirksworth, especially on market days.

The route through the Ecclesbourne valley is quite beautiful, passing between low rolling hills scattered with spinneys and copses. Charcoal burners could be seen at work from the train in the late 19th century, whilst another rural industry was carried on beside the river. This was clog block cutting and it took place in summertime amongst the alder trees growing thickly along the river banks.

Alder is soft to work with but extremely hard-wearing, and does not warp even after repeated wetting. For this reason it was popular in Derbyshire for domestic platters, but the wood was chiefly felled for clogs. Alder wood changes from white to red when cut, before fading to a pale yellow. Birch was preferred by willow cutters and other workers whose clogs were likely to get damp. Aspen was a good alternative to alder, similarly light and durable, but supplies were less abundant. In the reign of Henry V, supplies of aspen were reserved for making arrow-shafts. Anyone who used it for clogs or pattens risked a penalty of 100 shillings.

To the mill towns

Clog block cutters worked out in the open, under a tarpaulin hung from four posts in wet weather and burning yellow wood-shavings if they needed a fire. They sawed the alder into short logs before splitting them lengthways into rough chunks. These they trimmed into uniform clog blocks by means of a cutting tool resembling a scythe blade. It had a handle at one end whilst the other end turned on a swivel joint fixed to a crude bench. Blocks were mostly about 14 inches by 4 inches (36 cm by 10 cm) and 8 inches by 3 inches (20 cm by 7.5 cm), from which a wide range of sizes could be shaped.

The blocks were bundled into sacks and sent away to be finished off by clog makers, mostly in the mill towns of Lancashire and Yorkshire, although in the early 19th century clog and patten factories were to be found at Glossop, Chapel en le Frith, Chesterfield and Derby. The clog makers rounded off the blocks, shaping a sole and scooping a hollow in the top surface for the ball of the foot. They fitted a leather upper and the job was complete.

Back in the Ecclesbourne Valley, clog block cutters were already planning a year, or perhaps two years, ahead, felling mature alder trees to be left to season. By late autumn the men had left, the cycle of their toil evident in piles of yellow shavings and freshly cut, bright red tree boles, until one year there was simply not enough demand to make it worth coming back.

An entry from the *Derbyshire Times* dated 2 December 1933 refers to Mr Daniel Thomas of Wirksworth as: "the only clogmaker left in the district." He had previously lived and worked in a tent in the woods but now, aged nearly 70, he shaped clog soles - as opposed to the basic clog blocks - from local alder wood, working in a barn on the Alton Hall estate.

Clog block cutters

COAL MINING

Isolated beds of coal occur close to the eastern and western boundaries of the Peak National Park. Though mainly of inferior quality, this coal was worth extracting from an early period, as indicated by an entry from *Annals of Coal Mining and the Coal Trade* (Galloway 1898): "Sea coal in the Forest of Macclesfield was committed to the charge of a forester appointed in 1382." (The term sea coal was used to differentiate from charcoal.)

Miners were lowered by rope into bell pits, so-called from their shape. Thirteenth/fourteenth-century Derbyshire mining records mention a woman killed by fire-damp (methane) and a man who fell to his death from a rope. According to a reference of 1815, a bell pit formerly existed near Stanedge Pole, Hathersage.

A geological survey map of 1852 shows Moss Coal Pits, Deep Sick Coal Pits and 'Coal' at Barber Fields, Ringinglow. Writing about this area in 1950/1, G.H.B. Ward describes surface evidence of shale and 'pudding hole' bell pits almost opposite the Ring o' Firs. Further up the Upper Burbage Bridges road, Ward found further 'pudding holes' and later workings where a shaft was sunk.

Tom Tomlinson quotes local recollections of: "... a smallholder who had a team of packhorses and who used to go up on top of a hill called Stanage, near a village called Hathersage, where coal had been found. This was called 'slack coal' and this neighbour took his team of packhorses and filled the double panniers on each one with this 'slack coal' and my father put it inside the big barn. On winter nights, the peat fire was banked up with 'slack coal' and this kept it in until the morning."

A coalmine at Fernilee in the parish of Hope was the subject of an ownership dispute brought before the Star Chamber in 1606. This mine was possibly submerged by the Goyt Valley reservoirs in modern times, along with a private mine that had served Errwood Hall. Several generations of the Shallcross family of Fernilee benefited from ownership of the High Peak coalmines, generally known as the Shallcross Pits, near Chapel en le Frith. One descendant, John Shallcross, issued his own trading tokens.

Coal seams around Axe Edge were worked from about 1600. Known collectively as the Buxton coal mines, though actually in the parish of Hartington Upper Quarter, individual titles included Goyt Colliery,

Goyte's Moss Colliery, Burbage Colliery, Axe Edge and Thatch Marsh Colliery, and the Level Mine. Extraction also took place in the 18th/19th centuries in Wildboarclough parish and Goldstitch Moss, Quarnford. Coal from Pott Shrigley served the local brick making industry in the latter half of the 19th century.

Collieries have also been worked at Rowarth, Robin Hood near Baslow, Beeley Moor, Lumsdale near Tansley, Tansley Green, and Chatsworth Old Park. The Baslow coal seam actually outcrops on the floor of the Emperor Lake at Chatsworth. In 1760 the sum of £7.4s was paid for sinking three pits "on the top of Chatsworth Park to try for cole." A further sum of £2 was paid to sink a pit 11yds deep in 'ye Park'. A coal tunnel in Chatsworth gardens has recently been made accessible to visitors.

Coal exposures at Alderwasley were exploited from at least the 17th century. During the Civil War Parliamentary troops "took pewter and brass out of a coal pitt worth £30." This may refer to valuables hidden for safekeeping but brass was also the name given to iron pyrites, found in certain coalmines. By his will of 1771, William Peat of Alderwasley bequeathed to his children "my Coal Pits or Coal Mines and Delphs of Coal and ... the Tools materials and utensils for the getting of Coal."

The lime burners

Coal extraction was most active in the Peak between 1780-1880 both for domestic use and, more importantly, as an alternative to the over-exploited supplies of wood and peat used in fuelling lime-kilns. (see Lime Burning) The availability of coal from the Goyt and House Coal seams, west of Burbage, and Axe Edge, led to the concentration of lime burning in the vicinity, notably on Grin Hill. This activity was also carried out on farms for individual use. Farmers from Monyash, Flagg, Taddington, Ashford and Wormhill collected coal from the Level Mine for this purpose. In 1780 the Duke of Devonshire, owner of the Buxton mines, leased coal rights on Goyt Moss to a group of four men, presumably lime burners, in return for the spreading of lime on his lands within Hartington parish.

The House Coal seam was worked by 130 pits between Berry Clough and the Staffordshire boundary. The most economical access to such a shallow seam involved sinking new pits and abandoning old ones. Deeper seams were reached by shafts or horizontal adits driven into the hillsides, known as 'day eye' pits. Small boys were put to work where space was restricted. Boys also led the horses that turned the gins, or horse engines, used for raising coal to the surface before the days of steam power. In 1790 the monotonous task of walking a horse in never-ending circles earned a lad six pence a day, a quarter of what a man was paid for underground maintenance or shaft sinking. Some later pits on the House Coal seam still show traces of circular tracks trodden into the ground by horses.

From around 1770, coal from Buckett Engine Pit on the House Coal seam was taken out by boat on an underground canal. The lad who boated the coal was paid eight pence a day. The canal had been driven towards, and then alongside, the coal seam. Known as the Duke's Level, it drained into the nearby River Wye. The outfall was put to good use in the 1880s when it was piped to a sewage treatment works in Ashwood Dale.

By the early 19th century, coal was being transported on the Peak Forest Canal, supplying many lime-kilns along its banks en route. The Peak Forest Tramway was busy with two-way traffic: coal was taken up to quarry workings around Dove Holes, and limestone and lime brought back down.

Meanwhile, a tunnel had been driven into Thatch Marsh Colliery by the Duke of Devonshire "for the better supply of Buxton with coals." Coal from the House Coal and Goyt seams was brought out through this tunnel on rails. Some time after the Cromford and High Peak Railway opened in 1831, sidings were constructed to deliver coal from Thatch Marsh and other collieries to quarries along the line.

The mines fell into decline as the new mainline railways brought in better quality coal from outside the Peak. The Goyt and House Coal seams were abandoned in 1893 and 1919 respectively. Their combined output had peaked at 31,300 tons in 1871, falling by 1891 to 10,200 tons. Ten years later just 1,100 tons were extracted from the House Coal seam.

In the past century, some old mines were accessed in times of national emergency. During the General Strike of 1926, for instance, coal from Axe Edge was supplied to the Magpie lead mine at Sheldon, and stories are told of coal again being extracted when the severe winter of 1947 led to acute fuel shortages. That was the year when coal mining companies were nationalised, but in the Peak there was nothing left to take over.

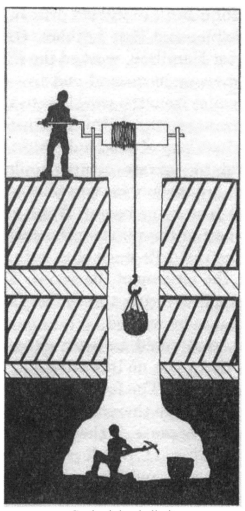

Coal mining bell pit

COOPERAGE

According to Pliny, the making and repairing of wooden casks or barrels, a craft known as cooperage, originated amongst the inhabitants of the Alpine valleys and was known by at least Roman times.

The familiar barrel shape is achieved by enclosing a circlet of vertical curved staves within horizontal hoops, narrower at each end with its greatest diameter in the middle. Used as a means of transporting produce, even a heavy cask is easy to control by rolling.

Tubs, churns and wooden pails - known in the Peak as kits or piggins - come together under the term 'white cooperage', while casks are described as either slack or tight. Slack casks have been used for transporting and storing a vast variety of produce, from fruit to fish and china to cement. Slack casks tend to be made from soft woods, mainly fir.

Well-seasoned oak is preferred for tight casks, as used for wine, cider, ale, oil, and liquid chemicals. Tight casks require accurate assemblage to make them perfectly watertight and also capable of withstanding internal pressure produced by fermenting liquids. To this end, the edges of each stave are bevelled to form tight joints with those adjacent. During manufacture by traditional methods, the bevelled staves are first steamed or heated to make them flexible, then arranged upright inside a circular frame. Held in place by temporary hoops, the upper ends of the staves are drawn together (formerly by a rope attached to a windlass) while permanent truss hoops, commonly made of iron, are dropped into place. The cask is upturned and the process repeated. Each end of the cask will have been prepared with a croze or groove to take a flat tight-fitting lid, known as a head.

Early trade directories refer to coopers in numerous villages and towns around the Peak. Taking the year 1857 as an example, Ashbourne, Wirksworth and Cromford each had two, while individual coopers were at work in Youlgreave, Bakewell, Bonsall, Hartington, Tissington, Elton, Stoney Middleton and Wensley. Half a century later their number had been reduced dramatically, with only nine in the whole of Derbyshire, including one each at Ashbourne and Wirksworth.

Progress brought about the manufacture of barrels without separate staves, using instead a sheet of wood sawn from a log in one continuous wide strip to form a cylinder. By cutting V-shaped wedges around the ends, it could be shaped into a barrel which bulged at the centre. Steel has been used in more recent times for both straight-sided and barrel-shaped casks.

One historical anecdote refers to wooden casks put to treasonable use on the outskirts of the Peak District, when secret messages hidden in Burton beer barrels were sent to Mary, Queen of Scots, held captive at Wingfield Manor. This desperate tactic was part of the conspiracy that led to the execution of Anthony Babington of Dethick, and ultimately of Mary herself in 1587.

From Haddon comes the story of a massive tree known as My Lady's Oak, felled in Haddon Park in 1728. The bark was sold to a Bakewell tanner for £5.15 shillings before four cords (one cord = 128 cubic feet) of top wood were removed. The remainder, an estimated 960 cubic feet of solid oak, was purchased by Henry Green of Whittington and Thomas Gardom of Baslow for £5.16 shillings. They sold a couple of lengths and the rest was hewn into coopers' ware by Robert Jenkinson, who managed to produce "914 large bottoms, 500 kit bottoms, 460 each of pannel piecings and short ware, 160 piggin bottoms and 3360 kit staves." After paying Jenkinson almost £6 for his labour, Green and Gardom were hardly left scraping the barrel, so to speak, pocketing a net profit of around £74.

COPPER MINING

Although pockets of copper ore were found in certain lead mines, copper mining in the Peak was neither widespread nor generally worthwhile, with one important exception.

A number of small copper mines were worked in the locality of Butterton and Onecote, Mixon mine being the most productive, but the richest output by far came from nearby Ecton Hill in the Manifold Valley. In its heyday Ecton was, perhaps, the richest source of copper in Europe and the mining rights belonged to the Earls, and subsequently Dukes, of Devonshire. The geological description of the hill is carboniferous limestone in an anti-cline with its axis running north and south. Small quantities of lead and zinc have also been found in addition to beautiful specimens of a variety of minerals, notably dog-tooth spar containing crystals up to 3 feet (almost a metre) across. There are even unconfirmed tales of gold.

It is not known for certain when ore was first extracted at Ecton but the earliest documented activity took place in the early 17th century. At this time the privilege of mining copper in Staffordshire and Derbyshire belonged to the Company of Mineral and Battery Works. However, the proprietors of Ecton mine were openly flouting that monopoly, for in 1633 the Earl of Devonshire was accused of operating a mine on his lands without a lease. The Company instructed: "That the Earle of Devon be waited on or some agent of his spoken with to know by what Authority the said Earle worketh the said Myne." There was no response and the Company allowed the matter to drop, virtually foregoing any interest in mining operations at Ecton.

Tradition holds that Ecton was the first mine in Staffordshire to use gunpowder, also pre-dating any type of mine in Derbyshire. Its introduction has been linked to Prince Rupert, nephew of Charles I and a keen experimental metallurgist with a particular interest in gunpowder. He was also governor of the Company of Mineral and Battery Works, referred to earlier. When this body abandoned its influence at Ecton, so, ipso facto, did Prince Rupert. He kept out of England during the Civil War, so if he really was responsible for introducing gunpowder to Ecton, it is difficult to say when.

Diabolical mansions

By the early 17th century, English copper mining had almost ceased in the face of foreign competition. Ecton, however, enjoyed a brief resurgence between 1660 and 1665 when just over four tons of copper were sent to London. J.A. Robey (*Bulletin of the Peak District Mines Historical Society* 1969) notes that in 1665 the mining lease passed to Jacob Mumma, believed to have been part-owner of a brass wire mill at Esher in Surrey. Copper, of course, is a component of brass. Surrey was also an important manufacturing centre for gunpowder and its introduction to Ecton may be linked to Mumma rather than Prince Rupert.

Attempts to resume mining around 1707 were short-lived, but in 1739 a Cornish miner, probably employed at a nearby lead mine, rediscovered copper ore on Ecton Hill. Together with 'some adventurers from Ashbourne' he obtained a 25-year lease from the Duke of Devonshire. Some of these speculators backed out but a fortune awaited those who took their place. After some £13,000 had been spent in sinking a shaft and driving a level, copper ore was found in vast quantities. The ore generally yielded about 15% copper and was worked in vertical masses called pipes, up to 70 yards (64m) across and widening out into vast bell shapes. Between 1760 and 1768 the copper yield was worth almost £57,000.

Not surprisingly, the Duke of Devonshire did not renew the lease in 1764, but took over the entire undertaking himself. An article by William Efford, published in the *Gentleman's Magazine* of February 1769, tells of a visit to the mine by the 4th Duke six years earlier. Access was by means of an almost level adit about 400 yards (366m) long and up to 6 feet (1.8m) high. Says Efford: "Thus far into the Mountain, with the aid of lights, 'tis easy enough of access. The late Duke of Devonshire ventured to this platform, took a cursory view of the works, gave the miners ten guineas to drink, but returned immediately not choosing to descend below. Indeed, such a horrid gloom, such rattling of waggons, noise of workmen, boring of rocks under your feet, such explosions in blasting and such a dreadful gulph to descend, present a scene of terror, that few people, who are not versed in mining, care to pass through." Efford adds that it was a further 160 yards (146m) down to the "place of action ... ten thousand times more astonishing than that above", where miners welcomed visitors to their "diabolical mansions" with a salute of half-a-dozen blasts of explosive.

Altogether more than 300 men, women and children were employed, including 60 miners earning a shilling (5p) per six-hour shift.

They descended to the workface on wooden ladders or stemples - lengths of wood fixed across the shaft - with candles stuck into wet clay for illumination. The ore was raised in tubs and the largest pieces were smashed by men with sledge hammers before being barrowed to a shed, where young girls sorted it into three grades. In another shed about 50 women crushed the graded ore into finer pieces using flat hammers called buckers. The girls earned between two and four pence a day (1-2p) and the women between four and eight pence (2-4p).

The crushed ore was buddled (washed) in buddling pools. A water powered stamps mill opposite Swainsley Hall later took over the crushing work, giving name to Stamps Bridge, better known today as Ecton Bridge. Finally the good ore was heaped up and auctioned off. The refuse ore was originally smelted on site, but in 1770 the Duke of Devonshire built a smelter at Whiston to serve the Ecton and Mixon mines. Transport to Whiston was originally by pack mules and horses via Grindon, Waterfall and Winkhill, where one section of track is still called Duke's Lane. Local farmers later acted as carriers using horse drawn carts.

The mines on Ecton Hill: Deep Ecton, Dutchman, Waterbank, Stone Quarry, Clayton, Good Hope, Gregory, Clay, East Ecton and Bag Mine, drew workers from a large area. This entry appears in the Grindon register of 1774: "1 August, buried Solomon Barker, kill'd ye 29th July, by a fall of earth in a level in Ecton copper mine." Tradition has it that Wardlow's parson used to preach to many of his parishioners in their work place, meaning that he held Sunday services down the mine.

Extensive remains

Abundant as the mine proved, it was virtually exhausted within a lifetime. And lucrative as it was for the Dukes of Devonshire, the story that Buxton Crescent was built entirely from the profits of Ecton is given little credence at Chatsworth. Nevertheless, total sales between 1760 and 1817 amounted to £842,351, of which £322,968 was profit.

Ecton had become one of the deepest copper mines in Europe - a 480ft (146m) shaft sunk in 1768 finally reached 1380ft (420m). Yet by 1820 only shallow workings were in use and 50 years later the output had dropped to just one ton a year. Extraction had ceased completely by the end of the century.

Many of the old buildings lay buried beneath waste tips that tumbled down the hillside. Foundations were exposed in more recent times as tips were cleared, mainly for use as road building material. As well as workers' cottages and mine buildings, there was formerly a cooperage, forge, carpenter's shop and a small school provided by the Duke of Devonshire.

Today the steep slopes of Ecton Hill are crossed by ramblers' tracks, offering a spectacular viewpoint with much visible evidence of mining activity, whether fenced-off, gaping shafts or ruins high on the hillside. The underground workings, with massive bell-shaped chambers up to 400ft (122m) across, became popular with cavers but now lie largely under water. Above ground, evidence of the old industry can be seen in two copper spires, one on a house at the base of Ecton hill, the other on Sheen church.

A postscript was added to the story in 1972, when the old Ecton mining rights were finally sold by the Duke of Devonshire.

CORN MILLING

For thousands of years we have been eating bread, so for thousands of years we have been making flour, or at least meal. Today's bread flour is primarily made from wheat. Only wheat and rye yield flour that forms a dough capable of aeration by using a leavening agent such as yeast, to give a spongy, light bread.

Neolithic farmers grew wheat and barley. Their meal or flour was produced by grinding the grain between two 'quern' stones. A number of prehistoric querns have been found in the Peak. Prehistoric flour was unrefined and gritty, contributing to the dental wear seen on skeletons and on a large number of teeth found in burial mounds at Stoney Low and Harborough.

Hand milling became a little easier with the development of the grist-mill, where grain was spread onto a large flat stone to be crushed by a stone roller. By medieval times, the work was carried out on a commercial scale, using two circular millstones turned by oxen.

Further progress came with water or wind power. Windmills were recorded in Britain from the 12th century onwards. Only an occasional ruin survives in the Peak. A windmill at the west end of Eyam was demolished some time prior to 1877, its stones re-used in building a school. An entry of July 1915 in *The Diaries of Maria Gyte* gives a rare reference to a windmill near Ashford: "Three women and a man came in horse and trap and had refreshment here ... They said they were the daughters and son of the late Wm. Gregory who between fifty and sixty years ago had a windmill at the top of Sheldon village."

The reason for the naming of Windmill, a hamlet near Great Hucklow, can only be an inspired guess since there are no known records relating to a mill here.

Water mills, in evidence since the latter part of the Roman occupation, were far more numerous. Even a fairly insignificant stream could power a corn mill. The Domesday Survey recorded many mills in the area now covered by the Peak National Park, including Bakewell, Ashford, Hope, Tissington and Youlgreave. This latter may have been the forerunner of the surviving and picturesque Alport Mill. Maria Gyte gives regular accounts of oats being taken to Alport (Johnson's) Mill for re-collection as oatmeal - a typical routine all around the Peak.

Frith Mill, on the Manifold near Longnor, was recorded as early as 1404 and replaced 200 years later by Longnor Mill. Out of use at various periods, it came back into service in 1831 and continued milling corn for another 40 years. A complete restoration is in hand.

Millers were entitled to keep a portion of flour in payment for their services but gained a general reputation for being dishonest and greedy. It gradually became more common for a farmer to sell his corn to the miller then buy back the processed flour.

Fine and white

As larger mills were built, occasionally up to 10 storeys high, the milling process became more complicated, with machinery keeping many men in work. Public taste was all in favour of progress: people liked their flour fine and they preferred it white. For this reason flour began to be bleached, at one time by chemical means but later by other processes such as the application of heat. Unfortunately, fine grinding and bleaching leave the end product less beneficial to our diet, but advice from nutritionists seems unable to reverse the trend.

Grinding by millstones has been described as the 'sudden death' method, subjecting the grain to shorter but rougher processing. The manufacture of millstones was an important industry in itself and great quantities were dispatched from Peakland gritstone quarries.

An improvement to flour quality came with the introduction of roller mills, better suited to the hard varieties of wheat. A fine working roller mill stands on the Wye at Rowsley, where John Caudwell built his first mill in 1874 on a site leased from the Duke of Rutland. The mill was originally powered by two water wheels, but in 1885 they were retired in favour of a revolutionary new roller system. The water wheels were replaced by turbines and the millstones by steel rollers. Caudwell's Mill remained with the family for over 100 years. Commercial production ceased in 1978 but the mill operates as a working museum and still produces strong flour for sale.

Further upstream, the Wye drove corn mills at Blackwell and Wormhill. This latter stood in Miller's Dale, to which it gave name, and was of ancient origin. In the early 13th century King John gave a mill at

Wormhill to Daniel Pincerna. Flewitt's Mill at Ashford and Victoria Mill at Bakewell, both on the Wye, ground corn for local farmers within living memory.

Cromford's manorial corn mill was replaced by one built by cotton magnate Richard Arkwright to provide 'his' village with flour. Fed by a millpond on Bonsall Brook, it remained in use until about 1930. At a higher point the tumbling brook once powered Bonsall corn mill, now just a scattering of ruins at the top of Clatterway. Until around 1900, the neighbouring hamlet of Ible boasted a working corn mill near the former Lilies Inn in the Via Gellia. The ruins lie beside an overgrown section of the stream.

Far more impressive is the ruined mill on the Derwent in Chatsworth Park. Designed by James Paine and built in 1761, it remained in use until about 1950 but was wrecked when two beech trees fell on it during a storm of 1962.

The River Dove was put to good use on its way through villages including Glutton Bridge, Hartington and Thorpe. The Dove still feeds a leat beside a converted mill at Hartington, now a dwelling with the attractive addition of a preserved undershot water wheel.

Quiet backwaters

Almost every sizeable flow of water was put to use grinding corn. A leat from Peakshole Water drove Castleton corn mill until the 1920s, apparently a different building to that referred to in a deed of 1615, granting two acres of waste ground near Castleton to Thomas Dixon and John Williams, Serjeants at Arms, to erect a corn mill on the River Ashop. Castleton had three corn mills by the late 18th century. A mill at Curbar relied on the Barbrook, and one at Highlow on Bretton Brook. The unassuming River Noe was the force behind Brough corn mill, where two water wheels worked five sets of grindstones. Threshing was carried out on site and the grain was dried in a kiln ready for grinding.

Middleton Mill near Youlgreave lay on the River Bradford, its exact position uncertain. What may have been the original corn mill burned down in 1733. It was obviously rebuilt, for in 1807 an inquest was held into the death of the miller, William Fletcher, who had become fatally entangled in the machinery. A large new mill was built on the site in 1822 and dismantled some time before 1914. The stone was used to build Castle Cottages in Middleton.

A number of corn mills were superseded by ambitious larger buildings for industrial uses such as cotton spinning, as at Calver, Bamford and the Brund Mill at Sheen. Carter's corn mill at Stoney Middleton became a footwear factory and Wetton mill, a farm. Peak Forest, Hope, Padley and Leadmill at Hathersage are just a few places where former mill buildings have been converted to residential use, while traces of old abandoned corn mills are evident in mill pools, weirs, leats and tumbledown stonework in quiet backwaters all around the Peak.

Old post mill

FLAX & LINEN PRODUCTION

Flax - *Linum usitatissimum* - has been cultivated since prehistoric times, possibly originally for food. Over time we learned that flax could produce both linen fibre and linseed oil, making it an important crop plant, sown in spring and harvested after about three months.

Linen was manufactured in Derbyshire during the Middle Ages. The later import of linen cloth led to an Act of 1533 obliging arable farmers to sow a fixed quantity of flax or hemp in proportion to their total annual tillage. Before the advent of machinery, the flax plant was pulled from the ground by hand, dried, de-seeded by hand-threshing and retted (partly rotted) by immersion in water, usually a pond or slow-moving stream. This softened the woody stem, enabling the outer bark to be peeled away to expose the core containing the fibres. Short or tangled fibres would be spun into coarse yarns for cord and twine, leaving the finer yarn for linen.

This completed the process of dressing, a fairly commonplace rural industry. We find a Winster boy apprenticed to a Bonsall flax dresser in 1760, and a flax dresser by the name of Joseph Hall living at Castleton in 1828.

Flax was also grown and processed by householders, often providing sufficient quantities of yarn to make all the linen needed for their own apparel and domestic use, from sheets and towels to shirts and smocks. The following relates to domestic life in Ashford in the 18th century: "The mistress of each home, and her daughters, as well as the female servants, might all be seen on winter evenings busily engaged in spinning flax into yarn. Spinning wheels were then as common to a domestic establishment as chairs and tables are now. A marriageable female at that period was expected to possess, if no other portion of this world's riches, an entire stock of linen for clothing and house use *of her own spinning*, hence the origin of the word *spinster*."

This explains an entry in Leonard Wheatcroft's journal of May 12, 1733: "Hanna [his daughter] came from Unston to spin against she was married, and Monday the 25th June she was married."

The Ashford recollections continue: "While the spinning wheel was in use amongst families, various trades were carried on in the village and neighbourhood, rendered necessary from the use of the wheel, [such] as a tow heckler, to prepare the flax for spinning; a dyer for the yarn that required colouring; a bleacher, with a whitening croft, for the yarn intended for white articles; and a linen weaver, to complete the business of cloth making for use. The tow heckler, the dyer, the bleacher, and the weaver, all of them once enjoyed local habitations and local celebrity in the village."

By the mid-19th century most spinning wheels lay still, the winter evenings' employment at an end. Cotton had superseded flax, outdating Acts of Parliament introduced under George III, when duties were imposed on foreign linen to provide bounties for growing British flax and hemp. A further act of 1782 allocated £15,000 out of these duties towards a bounty of 3d per stone for dressed hemp and 4d a stone for dressed flax. The initial act expired after five years but was renewed for a further seven.

Claimants to the bounty had to comply with strict conditions. Preparation of the raw material needed to be carried out properly, with parish officials signing a certificate giving a full account of the sum claimed plus details of the exact field where the crop was grown. The certificate had to be endorsed by a Justice of the Peace and the claimant was obliged to enter into a bond of treble the value of the bounty.

The 'Equalinum'

Flax spinning was moving towards industrialisation. In the 1790s, two brothers, Edward and John Dakeyne, of a flax manufacturing family in Darley Dale, invented a flax spinning machine. They called it the 'Equalinum' and took out a patent in their father's name as both sons were under age. The brothers set about erecting a new flax mill of five floors with capacity for 20,000 spindles. This building was replaced or at least partly rebuilt in 1826. Four years later the Dakeynes invented an ingenious 35h.p. disc engine to drive their mill machinery. Described as a "Hydraulic Engine for communicating motion to machinery", it was powered by a fall of water fed by a flight of four dams on Sydnope Brook. An additional use for the new machine was recorded in 1833: "A house organ is now erecting under the direction of Mr John Dakeyne, of Darley, the bellow whereof is intended to be put into action by the said patent machine."

The enigmatic motto on the Dakeyne coat of arms reflects their business interests even if its meaning is something of a puzzle: 'Strike, Dakeyne, the devil's in the hempe.'

45

Flax spinning mills also operated at Upper Hulme in Leekfrith and Gradbach in the parish of Quarnford. Flax was widely grown on farms on the Staffordshire side of the Peak over a long period, originally for spinning in local homes. Every process of production and manufacture was once contained within the parish of Wetton, whilst a linen weaver was recorded at Alstonefield as late as 1851.

According to Farey, the plant was grown in useful quantities at Brassington, Crich and Alton near Ashover. The place-name Flax Butts at Eyam suggests production there, similarly Flax Dale at Middleton by Youlgreave and Flaxdale Holding near Parwich.

Demand for linen may have fallen against cotton and synthetic fabrics but it remains popular for certain clothing and domestic items. Leading producers in modern times have included the former USSR, Romania, Poland, Germany, France, Belgium, Holland and, most famously perhaps, Ireland.

Cloth dressers

46

FRAMEWORK KNITTERS

The history of hand-knitted clothing in England goes back at least five centuries. Knitted woollen caps were such an important commodity in the reign of Henry VII that prices were regulated by an Act of Parliament. Knitted hose, however, was as yet unknown, stockings being made from cloth cut to shape and seamed at the back.

Silk stockings began to reach England in Tudor times. Henry VIII and later his son, Edward VI, were each given a pair of long Spanish silk stockings which drew much admiration at Court. Their successor, Elizabeth I, was presented with a pair of black silk stockings in the third year of her reign, from which time she refused to wear cloth hose ever again. It was one of her subjects, a Nottinghamshire curate named William Lee, who around 1590 invented a hand loom known as the stocking frame. Within less than a century, knitting in silk was a well-established cottage industry located principally in Derbyshire, Leicestershire and Nottinghamshire.

The skill could be mastered within six months and the vast majority of framework knitters, or stockingers, were women. They commanded good pay, producing garments for the hosier who supplied the raw material. Some workers saved to buy their own frames but many rented from capitalist hosiers who owned as many as 100 frames.

By the 18th century, framework knitting kept whole families in employment in their own homes. Even young children could help, winding hanks of yarn onto bobbins ready for use and seaming the finished goods. Workshops were established on the upper floors of some workers' cottages, with long windows running the length of the wall.

The range of silk goods extended beyond stockings to scarves, neckties, shirts, vests and underwear. Changing fashions called for mittens, 'ladies dresses' (a style of underwear later known as combinations) and tasselled smoking caps for gentlemen. Silk framework knitters continued to command the best pay when fine cotton yarn came into use, boosted by the invention of Jedediah Strutt's 'Derby Rib' - a machine for making ribbed stockings - in the late 1750s.

Rapid manufacturing growth followed the introduction of 'wide' frames. Whereas the old narrow frames produced fully-fashioned, i.e. shaped, stockings, wide frames turned out 'cut ups'. For these the cloth was cut, soaked and stretched to shape on a leg-board. Cut ups were not particularly hard wearing and lost their shape after being washed, but they were cheaper to buy. Ready-made stockings were now affordable to the working classes, previously familiar with only hand-made woollen hose. And on the wider scene, a change in fashion from knee-breeches to full-length trousers meant that shape was less important than price.

Stinting and trucking

As usual, industrial progress brought grievances. Alongside competition from cut ups, the introduction of machinery and a move towards factory production made great numbers of home knitters redundant. This was a primary cause of the Luddite riots of 1811/12, directed specifically at wrecking stocking frames. To make matters worse, stockingers were in the hands of hosiers who rented out far more frames than could be kept fully employed. This resulted in 'stinting', whereby available work was shared out without any compensatory reduction in frame rents. To boost their falling income, knitters put in longer hours and often at least doubled their output. The result was a vicious circle of over-production and shortage of work.

Yet another cause for complaint was the system of 'trucking', under which a hosier's middle-man, invariably a shopkeeper local to the workers, paid them not in cash but in goods - frequently overvalued or of poor quality - or further supplies of raw yarn. Framework knitters' petitions to Parliament merely drew advice. The following suggestion arose from a Commission of 1840: "... enlighten the handloom weavers as to their real situation, warn them to flee from the trade and to beware of leading their children into it." A Royal Commission of 1845 concluded that the industry could survive only through reductions in labour and productivity.

The problem of over-manning began to ease as workers found new jobs in the expanding factory system. The remaining streamlined workforce of stockingers gradually became financially viable and in the 1860s formed their first trade union. Large numbers of married women became outworkers, using single frames in their own homes.

Outwork thrived at Bonsall over many generations. A well-lit workshop with a datestone of 1737 survives in Bonsall Dale, once the home of William Oliver who worked there as a silk knitter all his life, operating up to 24 frames. For a time he worked for Brettles of Belper, who at the end of the 18th century maintained 5,000 hand frames in outworkers' cottages, and later for the famous John Smedley Mills at Lea. William Oliver died in 1872 in his 80th year. His workshop was later re-opened by his daughter, Mrs Sheldon, who, with at least three other Bonsall stockingers, worked for I. & R. Morley of Nottingham.

A larger 19th-century workshop stands just above Bonsall Cross. Formerly housing six knitting frames, it was one of the last to remain in use into the past century. A stockingers' shop also survives on Royal Oak Terrace in Crich, complete with its expanse of windows. Crich and Fritchley together had 245 frames at work in 1844, involving more than 100 families producing cotton hose.

The typical long windows seen at Bonsall and Crich were essential for the intricate work carried out within. Additional lighting often took the form of oil or tallow lamps, frequently placed to shine through round glass globes containing water so as to concentrate the light. In some areas the water was coloured blue to gain a closer imitation of daylight.

Such are the memories which died with the last generation of stockingers.

GOLD & SILVER MINING

Gold and silver mining barely qualify as bygone industries of the Peak; nevertheless both have taken place on a limited scale.

The existence of local silver was known in early times and small amounts have been found in Roman pigs of lead cast in the Peak. The Domesday Survey refers to dues of £40 of pure silver collectable from the manors of Darley, Matlock, Wirksworth, Ashbourne and Parwich. But where did this valuable metal come from? Sixteenth-century records mention the existence of silver in the Nester lead mine on Masson Hill, Matlock, and in 1656 troops were sent to Youlgreave when lead miners threatened violence to outsiders who wanted to search their workings for silver.

The extraction of silver from Ball Eye lead mine, near Bonsall, was well organised and worthwhile: claims were made of up to 20 ounces of silver per ton of lead. Glover refers to a tankard, salver and two small tumbler cups produced from this source, all at one time in the possession of Mr Milnes of Ashover.

The process of separating silver had been abandoned at Ball Eye mine by the early 19th century. Recovery of silver from a lead mine was generally so wasteful to lead that it was not cost effective. Other lead mines which revealed silver include Millclose at Darley, Odin at Castleton and Mill Dam at Hucklow, whilst minute particles accompanied the find of gold at Ible in the 1940s.

Peakland gold

Claims for gold have been made at Wirksworth, Miller's Dale and Bakewell but the best known 'gold strike' in the Peak took place at Over Haddon in 1854, at a lead mine on the left bank of Lathkill Dale. Low levels of gold were identified in the presence of iron pyrites, otherwise known as fools' gold, in an outcrop of basalt lava.

Samples were sent to London for analysis and on 24 June 1854 the *Illustrated London News* reported: "The Derbyshire gold-diggings, of which the Crown is the owner, promise to be worth looking after. The stuff analysed contains twenty-five ounces of silver per ton, and an ounce and a half of gold."

Mining companies took an immediate interest. One venturer wanted to erect a crushing mill in Lathkill Dale, but permission was refused and the machinery was set up in an old mill at Brough instead. Investors in the mine watched their £1 shares soar to £25, then £30. Those who sold out then were the only ones to make a profit from Peakland gold. Quantities proved so sparse as to make the venture unrealistic. All the speculators pulled out and the Brough crushing mill was sold for £30, at a loss of almost £700. Many years later, an old man used to tell how he had found a nugget as big as half a pea in Lathkill Dale, and even today the locals can still point out their 'gold mine'.

Just over 70 years ago a young geologist named John Wells surveyed for gold in the Peak and was quoted in the *Manchester City News* of 17 June 1933 as saying: "There is gold in the Derbyshire Peak District - at a spot very well known to thousands of Manchester hikers. It is going to be our business to find it."

There the story seems to have fizzled out, but 11 years later a scanty vein was found in a basalt quarry in the Via Gellia below Ible. In *A Lifetime of Adventure*, published in the *Peak Advertiser* of 9 September 1996, Matlock man Cyril Goodall told how in the 1940s he was commissioned to prospect for gold near Grangemill, not far from Ible. The Barmaster supervised the adherence to old mining laws and Cyril was allowed to sink a 200ft (60m) lined shaft. The search was not quite in vain, although only sparse traces of gold were found.

Local gold made the headlines in 1992 when analysts at Sheffield University confirmed that volcanic lava from Matlock Bath contained gold at 37 grammes per tonne, a fairly respectable quantity. The lava samples came from Temple Mine, a former fluorspar mine kept open to the public by the Peak District Mines Historical Society. Dr Lynn Willies of the Peak District Mining Museum predicted: "For the area as a whole it might be a key for some of the future mining", though he warned that the law was "horribly complicated" as far as gold mining was concerned.

Meanwhile, the opportunity to pan for gold has proved very popular with visitors. At the end of the day though, the mineral wealth of the Peak is of a more useful variety than what we perceive as precious metals.

HAT MAKERS

The manufacture of hats in the Peak was of considerable importance to one place in particular - the village of Bradwell. Its speciality was the 'Bradda Beaver', the sturdy working headgear adopted by lead miners in the Peak and elsewhere. Perhaps a touch of rustic humour gave name to the style, since only the well-to-do wore top hats of real beaver fur.

The hat industry of Bradwell was therefore heavily dependent on lead mining, which it followed into decline from the latter half of the 19th century. Hat making was carried on in Bradwell for at least 100 years. During the industry's heyday around half a dozen workshops were in operation on The Hills and Smalldale alone. Eight hatters were recorded at Bradwell in 1820. One of their number was William Evans of Smalldale, who derived considerable wealth from the trade. At his death in 1844, aged 72, he left the rents on certain lands to be paid to the preacher of the 'old Chapel'.

The Middleton family of Bradwell had especially long associations with hat making. Job Middleton, an octogenarian at his death in 1899, owned a factory on The Hills, now a pair of limestone cottages. Job used to travel around buying wool, his raw material, no doubt leaving his daughters, who worked with him, to keep an eye on the other employees. In 1905, just one solitary Bradwell hatter, Theophilus Middleton, remained to talk of the old days. He became a hatter around 1875, one of a dozen villagers engaged in the industry full time. After he retired through ill-health he continued to live in his compact 'shop' with his wife. It had been her job to wash and card the wool. Her carding machine was a primitive arrangement of two flat boards about 10in (25cm) by 6in (15cm) covered with 'wire card' to clean and disentangle the wool. One board was fixed at the end of a kind of saw-bench. The operator sat at the opposite end armed with the second board, which had a handle, carding the pre-washed wool between the planks in preparation for 'bowing'.

This rather strenuous operation involved the use of a long wooden bow fitted with a catgut string. The work was carried out by Mr Middleton, spreading a quantity of carded wool onto a wooden hurdle then plucking the taut bow-string over the fibres. This caused them to rise and separate before settling into an even web. The web was consolidated into hard felt by 'planking', a lengthy process of alternately steaming the wool over boiling water and rubbing it so that it shrunk and thickened. Worked to the correct size, the felt was forced onto a semi-spherical wooden block and left to dry.

The shape of the Braddas, as the Middletons called them, resembled an inverted pudding bowl. They were finished off with a cotton lining and a band above the narrow, curled brim. Most of the hats were dyed black in a washing copper but some were left their natural colour. Braddas were thick and heavy, perfect for withstanding hard knocks and dripping water in the mines, while the crown was strong enough to support a tallow candle. The life of a hat was about five years and considered to be good value for money.

A hundred years ago, occasional orders from other lead mining districts continued to reach Mr Middleton. He still had a small stock of Braddas for sale although no new ones had been made for many years.

Hats for war

The process of making Bradda Beavers was little different to that used for hats made from animal fur, whether top quality beaver or cheaper rabbit or hare. This becomes evident from a description of working practices at Lea Wood hat factory near Cromford. This extensive hatter's mill complex centred on a three-storey building, the basement fitted with carding engines powered by a massive overshot water wheel.

The tedious job of planking was either given to out-workers or carried out in a planking shed on site: "... the workers would sit round a central cauldron of hot acidified water, alternately soaking and manipulating, rubbing and rolling the felt on the planks which surrounded the kettle into which any liquid drained to be reheated ... additional fibres were worked into the thin areas and especially to strengthen the brim" (Wigglesworth). Local people, mainly women, also made hats in their own homes on a self-employed basis.

Materials were mainly animal fibres such as fur, hair and wool. Large consignments of hats were sent to London to be finished off with peaks, linings, trimmings and ribbons, according to the latest fashion.

More than 100 people were employed at Lea Wood in the first half of the 19th century. In addition to turning out hats for the gentry, the workers made military caps and felt helmets for soldiers fighting in the Crimea. When the hatters themselves felt the effects of the Crimean War, through rising food prices, they were provided with a hand mill so they could grind their own corn.

53

Hat making was carried out on a smaller scale at Baslow and at Fritchley, where a row of houses retains the name of the Hat Factory. Between the 1820s/40s, hats were produced at Speedwell Mill in Wirksworth. An old mill at Brook House Clough, Rainow, was put to the same use until manufacture was transferred to Bollington around 1873.

Long after hat making ended in the Peak, the design of the old Bradda Beaver was resurrected in a manner that deserves wider recognition. It came about in the early days of the First World War when British soldiers at the front were in desperate need of suitable helmets. Research centred on the steel making city of Sheffield where, in 1915, Walter Sissons of W. G. Sissons & Company, silversmiths, suggested a pattern to the Munitions Committee. The die for the prototype was made from a plaster cast of an old Bradda hat, taken by Walter Sissons junior, who lived in Bradwell. The pattern met with instant approval and the Trench Warfare Department placed an initial order for one million helmets at 4s 6d each. For technical reasons, manufacture was transferred to a new plant in John Street, Sheffield, to be operated by Viners rather than Sissons.

The original dies survived until Sissons' factory in St Mary Street, Sheffield, was bombed during the Second World War - when British soldiers were once again fighting in helmets with that unmistakable Bradda-inspired silhouette.

Lace making

LACE MAKING

Lace making was unknown in England until its introduction by Flemish and French immigrants in the late 16th century, yet by 1662 import restrictions were in place to protect this fledgling industry.

Making lace by hand utilises narrow bobbins, the thread kept taut to follow a pattern previously pricked out on a tightly stuffed pillow. Bobbins were commonly made from bone or wood. The intricate craft of lace making lent itself mainly to women and children, working in their own homes for dealers who sold them the cotton thread and patterns then bought the finished pieces. Pay was poor, but girls as young as eight often worked 10-hour days. Yet by the time hand-made lace reached the customer, it was expensive and beyond the means of all but the wealthy. There was, nevertheless, high demand from the home market plus a considerable export trade to America, at least until the War of Independence (1775-83).

Changes came at end of the 18th century with attempts to mechanise the manufacture of lace-net. Parallels were drawn with the way the stocking-frame had revolutionised the hosiery industry, and in 1808 John Heathcoat of Duffield patented a water powered bobbin-net machine, an invention which used a twisted thread of cotton to produce a lace comparable to the hand-made product. The machine was well suited to the factory system, although attacks by Luddites prompted Heathcoat to move his own factory from Loughborough to Tiverton. One of his two partners established a successful factory at Derby, which operated until 1958.

A change from water power to steam power allowed machines up to 40ft (12m) long, determining the design of wide, multi-storey factories. Manual strength was needed to operate factory machinery, so the work mainly devolved to men, with women and children responsible for keeping them supplied with thread and pressing the finished fabric. Machine-made lace quickly found favour around the Midlands, especially at Nottingham, the traditional centre of hand-made lace.

Boosted by an invention that enabled patterns to be created in the lace, the industry expanded rapidly and workers were numbered in their thousands. Lace was now being produced by the length, and the demand for net curtaining accounted for a particularly high proportion of sales.

Royal princesses

A few enterprises were set up outside the major lace making centres. In 1840 two Chesterfield men registered a patent for "Improvements in the machinery used in manufacturing bobbin-net or lace." Six years later an inventor/manufacturer named John Walker Waterhouse was presented with a silver medal by the Prince Consort for his "Great lace-working machine at Chesterfield by which the finest Mechlin lace is produced." Waterhouse's wonderful machine performed almost a quarter of a million movements to produce a fine patterned lace, chosen by Queen Victoria for the Christening gowns of two royal princesses.

The occupation of lace maker appears in mid-19th-century census records of Middleton by Youlgreave, where a lace factory was in operation on the River Bradford, almost certainly connected with a nearby bobbin mill. (see Bobbin Mills) Middleton women had been making lace by hand for several generations but the number of home workers dropped off with the introduction of machinery. According to *Some Account of Youlgreave, Middleton and Alport:* "The lace was made in silk and cotton; in black, white and cream; in two qualities, the very fine and coarse; this was made on a specially made frame. The chief articles concerned were: Parasols, shawls, jackets, and narrow lace. An average wage of about 10/- [10 shillings, equivalent to 50p] to 12/- [60p] a week could be made, fine lace-making more than coarse. A parasol would make 6/-. One lace-maker of that period, being a skilled worker of fine lace, entered in a Paris Exhibition and won a first prize of 2/-, whereas her sister gained something higher, winning a special prize - that being a lace collar."

Although nothing remains of Middleton lace mill, its dam is still identifiable at the southern end of the Bradford, skirted by a public footpath.

Documentary evidence of a lace mill at Two Dales is sparse, but the late Mrs Linda Slack, a native of the village, recalled that lace was formerly made at Ladygrove Mill, now used by animal feed manufacturers S. & E. Johnson Ltd. Prior to 1882 this had been a flax mill (see Flax & Linen Production), so the change-over to lace must have been after that date. Mrs Slack's grandmother was one of 100 employees - some making lace, but others turning out such items as fur gloves made from rabbit skins, bought in locally. Both ventures were short lived and Kelly's Directory of 1900 lists no lace makers at all in the Peak, although manufacture of fine cotton lace thread continued at Edale Mills.

LEAD MINING

Lead mining is regarded as the oldest industry in the Peak, and the Peak District Mines Historical Society estimates that 2-3 million tons of lead ores have been recovered since mining began, probably in pre-Roman times. Aside from the thermal waters of Buxton, there would have been little else but lead to encourage a Roman presence in the Peak. Evidence of mining during the Roman occupation comes from some 20 pigs of lead bearing Latin inscriptions, and the discovery of lead ore on Roman sites such as the fort of Navio at Brough.

Early extraction was most likely by opencast methods where veins outcropped at the surface. Like others who followed, the Romans appreciated the special qualities of lead. Over time it came to be used for pipes, water tanks and roofing, weights, bullets and shot, and for lining fonts and coffins. Retired miners from the famous Millclose mine avow that lead exported from there in the 1930s went into making German bullets, soon to be used against British soldiers in the Second World War.

Tradition has it that work at Golconda Mine near Brassington, which continued well into the 20th century, began in Saxon times, while Odin Mine at Castleton is traditionally attributed to a Danish interest. Wirksworth lead mines came under Viking control in 874 when Repton Abbey, to which the manor of Wirksworth was attached, fell to Viking invaders who had sailed up the Trent.

Mineral dues were later invested in the Crown. Ancient laws and rights governing lead mining were set down at the Inquisition of Ashbourne in 1288. The Peak's lead mining region is split into individually owned 'liberties' in addition to the King's Field of the High Peak and the King's Field of the Low Peak, administered by the Barmote Courts. The Barmotes are the oldest industrial courts in the world, with a Barmaster and jury to apply mining law and settle disputes. Although there is now little business to conduct, the courts still sit at Wirksworth and Eyam. Wirksworth Moot Hall contains the standard ore-measuring dish presented to lead miners by Henry VIII in 1513.

The law allows anyone to search for lead on any land within the King's Field except for gardens, orchards, burial grounds and the highway. A miner can also use or divert the nearest water supply for washing his ore and can cut any timber needed for his work. These privileges are a measure of the importance of lead, but the names of some old mines reflect hopes which may not always have been fulfilled: Dream, Good Luck, Chance, Hazard, Providence, Tanner's Venture, Neverfear and God Speed.

Rise and decline

Derbyshire supplied much of medieval England's lead, which was also a major 14th-century export. Lead from the Peak was both sold and shipped at Hull. In 1336 the Sheriff of Derbyshire was ordered to purchase a quantity of lead for the King's use, to be sent to Hull for forwarding to the King's Receiver of Victualling at Berwick-on-Tweed. In 1683 the mayor and burgesses of Hull brought an action against a number of Derbyshire lead merchants, accused of depriving these officials of their accustomed dues by avoiding the common weigh house before sale. The merchants had instead been landing and weighing their lead privately, transported from ship to shore and back under cover of darkness. They successfully pleaded that they had already paid staple dues on their lead at an earlier stage of its journey, in York.

From the 18th century, the installation of pumping and winding engines enabled mines to be driven deeper to reach new sources of ore. Underground water was a tremendous problem and ambitious drainage soughs were constructed, most of which still flow freely. Hillcar sough, for example, the longest in Derbyshire at four-and-a-half miles, discharges into the Derwent at Darley Dale, and the one-mile Mandale sough into Lathkill Dale.

Lead production peaked during the Industrial Revolution. In 1851-2 two Acts of Parliament were introduced to update mining law, the first applicable to the High Peak, the second to the Soke and Wapentake of Wirksworth along with the Liberty of Crich and the combined Liberties of Eyam and Stoney Middleton, Tideswell, Ashford and Hartington.

A number of factors, including expensive drainage problems, were now making lead mining uneconomic and a decline set in. Bradwell was hit particularly hard by the depression as early as the 1830s, when inhabitants looked for ways to relieve the plight of indigent local families. A London newspaper reported that it was: "impossible to conceive the vast depth of misery which exists ... many of these poor sufferers had their children in bed when visited, whose bedclothes had not a vestige of either linen or flannel about them."

One major exception to the decline was Millclose Mine at Darley Dale, referred to earlier, where the Watts shaft was reopened in 1859. Expanding to become Britain's largest-ever lead mine, Millclose reached its peak in the 1930s with around 800 employees, though mining operations ended in the summer of 1940.

Mining activity has left its mark all over the Peak. Lead workings dramatically changed the face of the landscape around places like Wirksworth, Matlock Bath, Monyash, Winster, Bonsall, Castleton, Bradwell and Eyam. Many old miners' paths are now public footpaths and care still has to be taken where they pass close to disused shafts. These run into many thousands and were largely uncapped until comparatively recently. Shafts were open death traps for centuries. Sadly typical of mid-19th-century accidents around Bradwell were the deaths of several children who fell down shafts, including a 10-year-old boy out 'bird-nesting'.

Any fatality in a mine had to be investigated by the Barmaster, taking on the role of coroner. Between the 17th and 19th centuries, scores of deaths were caused by rock falls and drownings - three men were killed in one day at Haycliff Mine near Eyam. Darley Dale registers reveal that in July 1669 William Hodgkinson and Robert Sidwell were suffocated in a mine, and in 1830 four men suffocated in an incident at Maypits Mine, Sheldon, when rival miners lit a fire.

Peakland lead miners had a reputation for being extremely hard-working, with a fondness for cards and drinking. Ale was believed to give some protection against lead poisoning - though in fact plain water was just as effective at flushing the kidneys! - and miners gathered at inns with names like the Pig of Lead, Miners' Standard and Miners' Arms. Castleton miners filled their glasses to toast their luck with this hearty drinking song:

"Come fellows drink - drink, drink your fill,
Full soon we must gang up the hill,
Where Odin rich in shining ore,
Shall give us glasses - hundreds more,
Then luck to Odin - golden mine,
With metal bright, like the sun doth shine."

For anyone wishing to study the history of lead mining further, numerous records can be consulted at the Local Studies Library in County Hall, Matlock. Specialist information and mining memorabilia warrants a visit to the excellent Peak District Mining Museum in Matlock Bath. This is operated by Peak District Mines Historical Society, which has received wide recognition for its preservation of the Magpie Mine near Sheldon and a wealth of important mining relics.

Lead smelting house

LEAD SMELTING

Whilst nobody would envy the working life of a lead miner, his contribution to the industry was only half the story. Further processes awaited the ore once it was brought out of the ground, beginning with preparations for smelting. Over a long period this task was largely undertaken by women and children surface workers, who sorted and dressed the ore ready for buddling (washing), which separated the unimportant, lighter rocks from the heavier lead ore.

The ensuing smelting process extracted the metal from the ore and frequently took place some distance from the mine on a site that handled the output from several mines. The earliest smelters, known as boles, were set up on exposed hilltops where the prevailing wind acted as a 'blast' for the fierce fire needed to melt the ore. Simple in design, if wasteful compared with future improvements, a bole was basically a depression in the ground enclosed by a low wall with a windward-facing gap. Layers of ore and firewood were piled into the hearth for burning, and the melted lead was channelled out into moulds to solidify into pigs. One site that has given up old stone moulds lies by the Bar Brook, east of Baslow.

Tantalising inscriptions on Roman pigs of lead are believed to refer to a place or mineral field named Lutudarum, the site of which has never been identified. One pig bears the word LVTVDARES, abbreviated on other examples to LVT or LVTVD. The seven 'leadworks' listed in the Domesday Survey are thought to have been smelting works serving areas around the places referred to: Ashford, Bakewell, Crich, Matlock, and three at Wirksworth.

Former smelting sites give us the place-name Bolehill, as at Wirksworth, Eyam, Hathersage, Wormhill, Bakewell, Holmesfield and elsewhere. The names Burton Bole and Smelting Hill occur at Abney, while Smeltinghill Wood is found at Fallinge, south of Beeley. Tangible evidence of lead smelting lies in numerous old slag heaps, or waste, including the Bar Brook site already mentioned and several examples on Beeley Edge. Some bole smelters produced 'blackwork', a slag containing enough lead to be worth re-smelting. Charcoal was added to the fuel to obtain a higher temperature and the result was a hard metal much valued for shot making. The remaining slag made good road surfacing material.

Reliance on wind power was hit and miss, one simple advance being the use of foot-bellows to provide sustainable draught. Water power was introduced to lead smelting in the 16th century, using a water wheel to work large bellows. This innovation was taken up on the River Sheaf at Beauchief and drew considerable interest. By 1574 a smelting mill was in operation on the Derwent in Chatsworth Park, followed by others at Calver, Curbar, Stoney Middleton, Hazleford Bridge near Hathersage and a mill belonging to the Duke of Rutland on the Wye between Beeley and Rowsley. Ruins in Hay Wood at Froggatt are attributed to an 18th-century smelting mill, where a stream was diverted along stone launders to a water wheel installed at a lower level.

A major advance arrived in the mid-18th century with the introduction of the low arched reverbatory furnace, or cupola, by the London Lead Company, a Quaker firm attracted to Winster lead mines around 1720. Their first cupola was constructed at Kelstedge near Ashover in 1735.

Inside the cupola

Under the rounded dome of a cupola, ore and fuel (generally coal) were kept separate and a strong draught, provided by means of a flue and tall chimney, caused the flames to reverberate from the roof and hearth, blasting them over the ore to melt the lead. The liquid metal ran into a pot and the slag was raked out. Not only was a cupola much more efficient than a bole, it was far less detrimental to health. Poisonous vapours were cooled and condensed in the flue as they were drawn towards the chimney, preventing the type of emissions that came from open smelting. That method left the surrounding land 'bellanded' - in other words too toxic ever to be grazed again. As recently as 1966, a number of cows died from lead poisoning due to seepage and disturbance of old slag heaps on a farm at Hope.

In the latter half of the 18th century, the existing smelt mill at Barbrook was modernised with the erection of a cupola, as was the communal Lord's Smelt Mill in Middleton Dale. A second cupola, Storrs Cupola, was sited at Stoney Middleton, and three mine-owning brothers from Middleton built another below Eden Tree at Bradwell. Of three other Bradwell smelt mills, the one known as the Slag Works, at the bottom of the Dale, was the site of a tragedy in 1854, when sulphurous fumes caused the deaths of two workmen and two young men who had gone to their rescue. The Slag Works had a 360ft (110m) arched flue, of which dilapidated remnant lengths can still be traced running parallel to the road.

Cupolas were built at Harewood on Beeley Moor and Lumsdale near Matlock, where a well-preserved chimney stands amongst other industrial remains maintained by the Arkwright Society. An area of rough ground north-east of Hathersage marks the slag heaps of Callow Bank cupola. A smelting works at Alport closed down in the latter part of the 19th century, leaving underground flues large enough to walk through, crossing and ascending the hillside. From approximately 1879 to 1924, white, grey and red lead was produced at Brough Lead Works, where smelting and refining continued around the clock.

Stone Edge Smelt, close to the A632/B5057 junction three miles north-west of Ashover, is the most completely preserved Derbyshire smelt works in its original state. The B5057 is the old Winster/Chesterfield road, so the works was ideally situated to serve the lead mines of both Winster and Ashover. It was also close to a good main road and no great distance from the Chesterfield-Stockwith Canal. In the late 18th/early 19th centuries, the output from Stone Edge reached some 500 tons of lead a year. Abundant traces of former activity include an impressive square-built chimney dating to the 1770s/1780s - possibly the oldest industrial chimney in Britain. The aptly-named Cupola Farm is close by, on the equally appropriate Belland Lane.

The fortunes of lead mining and lead smelting rose and fell together. So it was that when production boomed at the famous Millclose Mine in the 1930s, a smelter was erected on site. Lea Lead Works, where ore was normally taken for smelting, could no longer cope. When mining ended at Millclose in 1940, the smelter was taken over by present owners H. J. Enthoven & Sons, whose existing smelter in London's East End was at risk of being bombed. Today Enthovens is the largest single site producer of recycled lead in Europe. Its annual output of around 75,000 tonnes is partly recovered from millions of scrap car batteries.

This company is therefore heir to one of the oldest industrial processes known in the Peak, a world away from the simple boles where the story of lead smelting began. By complete contrast to Enthovens, a Romano-British smelting hearth of probable 4th-century date can be seen in the Peak District Mining Museum at Matlock Bath, alongside later examples of pigs of lead and assorted moulds, including an example incised 'T. Hill, Bradwell, Derbyshire'.

LIME BURNING

Lime burning has a long association with the White Peak, where limestone occurs in great abundance. The process produces lime or quicklime, which has known many applications. It was used in plasterwork by the Egyptians about 4,000 years ago, and both Greeks and Romans used lime in making cement and mortar. This latter use was recognised in a Roman bath found at Buxton many years ago.

For hundreds of years lime has been of enormous importance in agriculture, where it is spread on the land to improve acidic soils. One of the earliest references to this practice appears in *The Boke of Husbandrye* written by Fitzherbert in the early 1500s. In the mid-17th century, 14 lime-kilns were recorded at Dove Holes alone, apparently used to meet local requirements.

Constructed of stone, the kiln was filled from the top with alternate layers of broken limestone and fuel - wood, peat or furze. The kiln was lit through an opening at its base, starting the slow burning process that reduces limestone to lime. After a burning period of five to 10 days, followed by a couple of days cooling, the chalky lime was drawn out from the bottom of the kiln.

One type of kiln, the pye kiln, was usually built by an individual farmer, sometimes on common land and for only intermittent use. Such sites are commemorated in the familiar field name of Kiln Close. After meeting his own needs, a farmer could sell any surplus lime to other farmers. From the 17th century, lime was also in demand as a flux in lead and iron smelting. Lime also had, and rarely still has, a domestic use. Mixed with water it becomes slaked lime, formerly applied as a whitewash on the walls of cottages and outhouses all around the country.

Lime burning depended on a reliable source of wood, but as supplies of timber diminished, burners turned to coal. By the early 17th century, coal was in use around Axe Edge, which had the twin assets of coal seams and developing limestone quarries. The region became a major lime burning centre, with many dozens of independent operators concentrated on Grin Hill, their numerous kilns interspersed with large hillocks of ash waste. The hillocks hardened as they weathered, and some were hollowed out by poorer workers into simple dwellings of up to four rooms. The only natural light usually came from the 'chimney', a round hole in the roof, but there was no rent to pay and in winter the occupants benefited from warmth emanating from the surrounding kilns. At least one resident lived into his nineties. Some ash houses were topped with turf and, to the astonishment of visitors, an occasional cow grazed on the low sloping roofs.

Murky volumes

No longer was lime burning confined to an occasional task on the farm, or even to 'sale' kilns that supplemented a farmer's income. Growing demand from manufacturing industries led to the construction of 'running' kilns, so-called because they were kept working round the clock.

From the late 18th century, Stoney Middleton had a deserved reputation as an unhealthy place, smothered by a constant pall of acrid smoke from large-scale lime burning. Cartloads of coal were brought from Sheffield and Chesterfield, returning with processed lime. Eyam poet Anna Seward told how natural pinnacles were broken off the towering rocks above Middleton Dale for the "... perpetual consumption of the ever burning lime-kilns." She added, "These were very impressive by night, emitting their livid flames which seem so many small volcanoes."

Small Dale left a similar impression on Ebenezer Rhodes: "The burning of lime here is a considerable trade; and the kilns used for the purpose are situated at the bottom of the dell, one side of which was formed by the rocks where we stood; of the other, aided by a transient light emitted from the fires of the lime-kilns, we caught occasionally an uncertain glimpse ... the whole dale indeed was one immense cauldron steaming with smoke, that at intervals was partially illumined by momentary gleams and flashes from the fires below - then curling into mid-air, it rolled over our heads in murky volumes."

Advances in transport further boosted the lime burning industry. The Peak Forest Canal and tramway were in use by 1799 and resourceful operators set up numerous kilns along the canal. Boatloads of stone and coal were brought in and cargoes of lime shipped out. The Macclesfield Canal opened in 1830, linking the Peak Forest and Trent & Mersey inland waterways. This opened up access to new markets, from the chemical and steel industries to a building trade faced with an endless demand for mortar to build mills, factories, warehouses and housing.

Lime burners were soon to take advantage of the railway, which in 1863 reached Buxton with a siding at Dove Holes. Lime-kilns were established alongside the track, while quarrying in Great Rocks Dale and

Miller's Dale expanded to meet demand. A limeworks opened in Miller's Dale in 1878, using a system whereby limestone and coal was tipped into the top of the kiln from wagons, and the lime shovelled out at the bottom, ready to be sieved and taken away. Work ceased in 1930. Two restored kilns survive but the vast crushing plant of 1914 is derelict.

More than 40 kilns provided numerous jobs at Peak Dale into the 20th century. There were the burners who managed two kilns each and whose wages depended on the amount of lime they produced; the drawers, or pikers, who extracted lime from 'eyes' at the base of the kilns; and the pickers who separated lime from the ash for loading onto railway wagons. A lad's first job might have been as a bull head knocker. A bull head was a stone not quite burned through and still hard in the middle. As much lime as possible had to be knocked off before the raw stone went into the waste.

Work at the kilns was dangerous and led to horrifying fatalities. A Peak Dale boy of 14 received fatal head injuries when he fell from a platform while wheeling refuse from a bin. One of many 'Tragic Deaths' recorded at Bradwell is that of John Storer who, in April 1876, "fell into a lime-kiln at Potts and Jackson's, Dove Holes, and was burnt to ashes. Nothing was found but his knife blade, a few buttons, and one or two small bones."

Limestone in the Buxton area is the purest in massive formation in the world, with giant plants supplying modern needs including steel manufacture, oil refinery, building work and road building. Yet the old, redundant field kilns have not completely disappeared from the landscape. Many can be seen from public footpaths, occasionally identified by means of an information board.

PAPER MANUFACTURE

The invention of paper is associated with the ancient Egyptians and their use of papyrus reed. This material was not a paper in the modern sense, but did give us the word 'paper'. Equal credit goes to the Chinese, who succeeded in making paper from bark and hemp about 2,000 years ago. Arabs introduced this knowledge to Spain in the 11th century but it remained unknown in England for another four centuries.

Over a long period, the main raw materials of English paper pulp were rags and straw. A ready supply of swiftly running water was essential for powering the pulping machinery and for mixing with the shredded raw material to make a liquid pulp. This pulp was drained, leaving behind soft sheets of tissue to be tightly moulded together in a simple press and dried as a single sheet.

As time went by, the trade began to rely heavily on cotton rags, mostly collected by rag-and-bone men. Supplies also had to be imported, but a crisis arose during the Napoleonic wars, as explained in a letter to *The Methodist Magazine* of June 1808 and addressed to "the worthy Females, Readers of the Methodist Magazine":

"The humble Petition of a Paper Mill sheweth that your Petitioner is a very laborious servant of the public, who has heretofore been supplied with food, consisting of linen and cotton rags from Hamburg and Italy; from which was made paper for the Methodist Magazine ... by which much good has been done, and the glory of the Redeemer's kingdom greatly advanced.

That for some time past owing to the present circumstances of the war, the supply of foreign rags has been stopped, which has deprived your Petitioner of her necessary food and left her and her family almost destitute ... Your petitioner humbly conceives that the inhabitants of the United Kingdom are not sufficiently careful to preserve their rags ... and, were the female reader each to see to the preservation of all their linen and cotton rags ... your Petitioner conceives that a supply of rags would, by their means alone, be sent to the mills."

The 19th century brought an ever-increasing demand for paper, especially for newspapers and books, and experiments were made with other possible pulp sources. Esparto grass from Spain proved to be useful, but the most successful raw material turned out to be wood pulp. Within a short space of time, wood pulp was providing practically all the nation's newspaper requirements. Some publications even maintained their own forests. One million tons of wood were used for paper production in 1900 and, although manufacture had become more mechanised since the Industrial Revolution, the basic principles of making paper had remained unchanged.

Great dimensions

The history of paper making in the Peak is strongly rooted in the north west of the region. One of the largest manufacturers was founded around 1781 in a mill at Whitehough, Chapel en le Frith. By 1829 Whitehough Mill was producing the largest-sized paper in the country and supplying the London press with newsprint for 'newspapers of very great dimensions'. This included the first issue of the *Illustrated London News*. The mill once produced a sheet of paper with an area of one acre - the largest single piece ever made up to that time.

Whitehough Mill was extended several times and in 1840 employed about 100 hands. In 1869 the business was bought by the Slack family to add to their other paper making interests. Slacks had operated at Hayfield since the end of the 18th century, developing the extensive Bank Vale and Swallow House Mills. The latter closed in 1910, but Bank Vale remained open and work took an unusual turn during the First World War by producing large amounts of special paper for making into waistcoats and trousers for the troops. Output also included assorted wrapping papers for such goods as surgical supplies, tobacco, hosiery and Sheffield cutlery. In 1927 the business passed into the ownership of Joseph Isherwood, continuing as a paper mill until 1988.

Nineteenth-century paper manufacture took place at both Dinting and Charleston, near Glossop, but neither mill enjoyed long-term success. Olive & Partington of Glossop, however, established in the 1830s, became one of England's largest manufacturers. By the end of the century the firm occupied two sites, the Turn Lee and Dover Mills, keeping more than 600 people in work. The firm held patents on many of its machines, processing upwards of 120 tons of paper per week from Norwegian timber. Seventy years ago the weekly output had risen to 340 tons, producing paper for high-class magazines, catalogues and books as well as fancy coated paper and wrappings of gold and tinfoil. The works closed in 1963 with the loss of 600 jobs.

A paper mill was built around 1790 at Allgreave in the parish of Wincle, on the mid-western side of the Peak. It stood on Clough Brook, a tributary of the river Dane, but within a few years both the original mill and its successor had been swept away by floods. Nevertheless another mill was erected, three storeys high. Local tradition holds that the riskiness of this third venture gave it the name Folly Mill. By 1825 it was in the hands of Thomas Hope, who operated another mill on the Cheshire bank of the river. Folly Mill produced coarse brown and blue wrapping paper for traders such as grocers and ironmongers.

Shopkeepers' brown paper was also made at Green's House Mill on a remote stream in the parish of Outseats near Hathersage. It was worked in the 1840s by Charles Ibbotson and in the 1850s by Charles Marsden. Production ended in 1887 and the two-storey mill was demolished, leaving traces of a 40ft (12m) by 20ft (6m) building and a large millpond fed by springs.

Rags and spatches

No traces remain of an early paper mill at Alport near Youlgreave. It was in use by at least 1761, the date of a documented reference to the sons of John Hall, paper maker of Youlgreave. The mill stood on the left bank of the Bradford on the site of the present-day garden of Brookside Cottage. The names of Francis, James and William Kenworthy were connected with the undertaking between 1816 and 1852. In 1848 the Alport Mining Company threatened to take William Kenworthy, their tenant, to court for unpaid rent of £6 per half year.

First-hand recollections of Alport paper mill are recorded in *Some Account of Youlgreave, Middleton and Alport* by Miss Fanny Thornhill Needham, born at Alport in 1847. Miss Needham had childhood memories of ragmen delivering to the mill, where she and her friends were allowed to go and choose the best pieces for dressing their dolls. She used to play at the mill in wet weather and was sorely disappointed when it was pulled down.

Another early paper manufactory was Masson Mill, built around 1771 on the Derwent in Matlock Bath by Robert Shore of Snitterton and George White of Winster. In 1772 the partners were granted the right to convey water to their mill for a period of 21 years. The following advertisement appeared in the *Derby Mercury* of 13 August 1779: "Writing

Paper to be sold. At the Paper Mill at Matlock, on Monday next the 16th, a large quantity of writing paper of different sorts - & also a quantity of linen rags and spatches, & several pairs of paper moulds."

The following year Shore and White sold the mill as a going concern to Richard Arkwright who, in 1783, built his third cotton mill close by. Masson paper mill was tenanted and in 1811 forty workers were turning out brown, blue and white paper from old rope, coarse cotton and white rags. Manufacture ceased at one period but in the 1850/60s the mill was producing cartridges and pasteboards. It was still in operation at the beginning of the 20th century under Simons & Pickard, who also operated Dunsley paper mill in the Via Gellia.

An interesting post-script to paper making relates to the production of millstones for grinding wood pulp. From the late 19th century such millstones were a speciality of Messrs Percy J. Turner Limited of Stoke Quarries, Grindleford. The exceptional wearing qualities of Stoke pulp stones found a market in Canada, America and Scandinavia. Similarly, quarries at Stanton in Peak exported to Poland, and quarries at Ashover to Scandinavia, a profitable diversification in the old-established export of Peak millstones.

PEAT CUTTING

The bleak and bare moorlands of the northern Peak are literally laid with peat, but long ago these same uplands were thickly wooded with oak, elm and lime. Then prehistoric farmers began a long, slow process of land clearance. Without trees, the denuded ground became boggy, providing ideal conditions for the formation of peat from decomposing vegetable matter. It can be found up to 15 feet (4.6m) thick in places.

Cut into oblong bricks and stacked to dry in the sun and air, peat loses its soft, spongy texture and shrinks to become brittle and inflammable. Fortunately, extraction never became a large-scale industry in the Peak, although peat was a useful fuel for localised lead smelting and lime burning. Demand dropped off from the early 17th century as coal became affordable with the construction of new roads and, later, canals. Peat continued to be used for domestic fuel over a considerable period.

Peat pits have been worked at Crookstone Moor, below Ringing Roger, and on Grindlow. The 70ft wide (21m) Back Dike, a trench on Ridge Nether Moor at Bleaklow, possibly marks the site of large pits referred to by Farey. An area of perhaps 30 acres was worked near Lockerbrook Farm above Derwent and 75 years ago was still referred to by older people as Rowlee Peat Pits. They provided fuel for several generations of families living at Hagg, Bell Hagg, Rowlee, Fairholmes and Lockerbrook Farms. Around a dozen people would work together in pairs, some digging the sods, some stacking and wheeling them away, and others heaping them up to dry. Peat was still being burned in the locality after many households had changed to coal. Willis Bridge of Lockerbrook was still fetching peat around 1910.

A description of communal peat digging at Edale in 1851 was relayed many years later to author Tom Tomlinson. One of the participants was 10-year-old Nicholas Tym, whose family had farmed at Barber Booth for many generations. The boy understood from his father that for many years the Champion family of Grindslow House, owners of most of the land and farms in Edale, had allowed the inhabitants to dig peat from Peat Moor for fuel. This right was called 'turbary' and Nicholas was told that this word was written around Peat Moor on the big estate map at Grindslow House. There was also said to be a clause relating to turbary on the estate deeds, indicating well-established usage.

Looking back to 1851, Nicholas Tym recalled how at the end of April, as soon as lambing was over, all the farmers and cottagers gathered early one Monday morning to walk up Peat Lane, carrying peat spades, cutters and prickers onto Peat Moor. Peat Lane was sometimes called the Sled Road because horse-drawn sledges often brought the peat down this way. All the children had a week off school to help and boys were kept hard at work beside their fathers, cutting away any overlying loose peat, then using the strength of their arms to push the cutter into the deeper layer, 10 feet (3m) deep in places and often wet. But it 'cut like butter' and was dug out in blocks of about 12 x 6 inches (30 x 15cm), the exact size being determined by the worker's spade. These blocks were simply called 'peats'. As fast as they were cut they were taken away by the womenfolk to be propped up, one against the other, and left to dry in neat rows known as 'footings'. The day's work finished in time to get back for milking.

Over the next few days there was the same early start. On the Friday afternoon Nicholas spotted old Bardsley, the schoolmaster, coming across the moor. The boy kept on digging with his head down as Bardsley stopped to talk to other children before finally stopping in front of the Tyms. He watched for a while and remarked with a laugh that Nicholas got on better with peat digging than with his school work. Both teacher and farmer knew which was more important for now, and old Bardsley would be given a supply of peats when they were taken down to the village.

On the last day the footings were gathered into huge piles, known as pikes, built up from flat layers of peats, all pointing downwards and inwards and narrowing off to be topped by a single peat. Gaps were left for the wind to blow through and the pikes were left to dry until after haymaking, or about the end of August.

When all the hay and corn was in, farmers took the wheels off their big haycarts and replaced them with sledge runners. The cottagers had smaller sledges and everyone made their way up the narrow Sled Road to Peat Moor. The Tyms used to bring down 10 loads and that just about filled their peat house. Some farmers had 50 loads and at least one household got through a load a week. Practically every house in Edale had a peat house where the new supply was piled to capacity, kept apart from the previous year's dry and raggy stock. This would be used up under the oven on baking days and under the copper on washdays.

Edale farmers always made sure that anyone too old or infirm to cut peat still received a share; nobody went without a fire in winter-time. This example of community support continued even when the railway brought coal supplies into the Hope Valley in the late 19th century. Instead of spending a week cutting peat on the moor, farmers simply took their carts to Edale station yard and filled them up with coal as needed. When the people no longer exercised their turbary rights, a wall was built to keep them off Peat Moor, the final chapter in an old Edale tradition.

Peat baths

A more recent description of peat cutting was recorded by George Mellor of Hollinsclough, remembering a fine day in June 1938 when Mr Tunnicliffe of Black Bank, near Quarnford, was "busy cutting peat out of the ground with a hay knife." The story continues: "He was cutting round a big square piece of peaty pasture ground; he kept cutting round in thin slices about a foot square and setting them up on edge in fours to dry while the weather was at its best; and when dry, he carted them across to the house to back the fire up at night all through the winter months."

Modern uses for peat centre on horticulture, although alternatives are now available, and peat baths for relief from gout, rheumatism, lumbago and sciatica - a popular therapy in continental spas.

Peat erosion has become a matter of grave concern. Blame has been laid on various activities, whether moorland manoeuvres by military vehicles in the First World War or controlled heather burning on the grouse moors. A report from the early 1960s concluded that burning on Houndkirk Moor had stripped 4-5 feet (1.5m) of peat, down to the bedrock in places. But a continuing problem in the Peak is erosion caused by walkers; this threatens a far more significant area than all the old peat diggings put together.

Transporting peat blocks

PIGMENTS AND PAINT MILLS

The manufacture of paint has progressed from an early secret art to an advanced chemical industry strongly dependent upon synthetic materials. The basic constituents of a fluid paint are solid pigment, to give colour, and a liquid vehicle such as a drying oil or water solution.

The Industrial Revolution introduced water powered grinding mills to pigment manufacture, the raw material being pulverised to a powder between millstones then finely sieved. Actual paint mills produced a stiff paste from the pigments and liquid medium, to be ground between two millstones then thinned to a working consistency. Some records make it difficult to differentiate between colour grinding mills and paint mills. For instance a 'paint grinding' mill formerly stood by Viator's Bridge in Milldale, whereas the Goytsclough Mill, powered by the Deep Clough stream and now demolished, was recorded as a 'paint mill'.

Pigments were obtained from naturally occurring substances; some of those common to the Peak were discovered in connection with lead mining activities. Along with alum, copper and zinc, lead was an important metallic pigment. The mines of Bradwell produced white lead, the common name for lead carbonate, sought as white pigment for paint since the fourth century BC. The use of basic lead sulphate, known as sublimed white lead, dates from only the mid-19th century.

One source of red pigment was red lead (lead oxide), also an important component of anti-corrosion paints due to its rust inhibiting properties. A fictional description of manufacture at Castleton appears in *A Family Tour through the British Empire* (1812): " ... the melted lead being first exposed to the open air, the surface is soon covered with a dusky skin, which is taken off and succeeded by others, till the greatest part of the lead is changed to a yellowish green powder. This is afterwards ground fine, then washed and dried, and thrown back into the furnace, where, by stirring it, so as to expose every part of it to the air, it becomes red lead."

Red lead was produced in Bonsall Dale throughout the 19th century by the Via Gellia Paint and Colour Company, an extensive concern that by 1893 was powered by both steam and a 32ft (9.8m) water wheel. A wide range of colours was manufactured and one department specialised in grinding paints in oil. The company had a healthy export market and around 1905 expanded into the former Ashford marble mill.

Coloured earths were ground further downstream of Bonsall Dale at Scarthin, in a mill where the water wheel still turns. Under Henry Wheatcroft the mill dealt with ochre of several colours, along with "blacks, ivory, blue and mineral, chromates, blue vermillionettes and numerous others."

Black-wad and cauk

Manganese ore was being processed at a kiln or furnace at Wensley by at least 1829. A blackish-brown pigment obtained from the ore of manganese was known in the Peak as 'black wad'. It occurred in lead mines at Alport, Brushfield, Elton, Great Longstone, Hartington, Hopton, Matlock Bath, Monsal Dale, Parwich, Winster and Youlgreave, and around 1830 was being recovered in small quantities from Carsington Hill mine. Black wad pigment produced an oil colour for outdoor use, especially suitable for painting buildings - and ships of the British navy. This latter application is attributed to a Winster man by the name of Dawson, who supposedly suggested it to the Admiralty.

Barytes, known in the Peak as 'cauk' or 'cawk', found use as an extender pigment in paint, giving improved brushing and storage qualities. It remains an essential component of many paints, especially for priming and sealing purposes. Barytes was washed at a colour mill in Monsal Dale and, with the lead sorted out, prepared for use as a pigment. It was also ground at Cadster Mill, Chapel en le Frith, listed as a paint and colour works in 1857. Millions of tons of barytes were extracted from Bradwell lead mines, largely from the New York vein and Moor Furlong mines.

Around 1840 the former Lord's Smelt Mill in Stoney Middleton was taken over for the crushing of barytes, and a Lumsdale stone crushing mill began producing lead-based paint materials in 1850. About 10 years later a disused cotton mill at Brough was converted for the manufacture of white, grey and red lead. The Brough works were later extended by the addition of a smelting mill and refinery. Moving onwards, a paint and dye factory took over much of the old Cromford Mill site in 1921. Nearly 60 years later the Arkwright Society purchased the disused land and buildings and has had to carry out a lengthy decontamination scheme to restore the site to use.

Pigment manufacture continues under Viaton Industries Ltd, whose High Tor Works on the Derwent in Matlock Bath was originally established for mining iron ore. When the ore became worked out in 1850 the water wheel was used to grind white lead. Around 50 years later the Via Gellia Colour Company took over, installing a turbine to drive four pairs of Peak stones, which for 20 years ground iron oxide. The subsequent crushing of bone char, a waste product from sugar refining, took place into the late 1960s. Today Viaton blends pre-ground, chemically-produced colour products for use in paving slabs and other cementitious products.

Millstones

PINS AND NEEDLES

The attractive village of Hathersage, with its healthy clean air, has not always been so. Extensive wire drawing took place at the heart of the village in the 19th century, and the associated trade of needle grinding made life very unpleasant.

The work of sharpening needles to a fine point on a grindstone was dangerously unhealthy, giving early needle grinders a life expectancy of 10 years from entering the occupation. The whole village also paid a price in grimy, dust-laden air, with minute metal particles eating into the glass and stone of buildings near the mills, not to mention the lungs of the inhabitants. Those who lived on higher ground considered themselves fortunate.

Wire drawing was one of the secondary metal trades dependent on the iron industry of east Derbyshire, where ironstone occurs in the coal measures. Iron smelting is recorded at Barlow as early as the 12th century. Iron was later put to use on the outskirts of the Peak, where the Hallamshire region of Sheffield developed as a manufacturing centre for scythes, sickles and knives. Sheffield, of course, became world famous for its cutlery, a trade now represented at Hathersage in the distinctive factory of David Mellor.

Sheffield brass foundries used to provide metal for the manufacture of brass buttons in Hathersage (see Button Makers), but this was on a small scale compared with wire drawing activity. The story of its development in Hathersage is very involved but its inception may date from a patent granted by Queen Elizabeth I in 1565 to Humphrey and Schütz for the "making of steele and iron wyer". Schütz is known to have established a wire drawing works at Hathersage.

An important early product as far as the Peak was concerned were sieves, or riddles, for washing mineral ore, chiefly lead. Hathersage was a main supplier of sieves to Ecton copper mines. (see Copper Mining) Sieves/riddles appear in late 18th-century accounts from Ecton, including a 1779 invoice from James Hodgkinson containing an interesting reference to wire brooms: "24 Sive bottoms of No 48 wires £12.16.0d; 12 Wire brooms £4.18.3d [and] 12 Ridles at 1s 2d per Ridle 14s 0d."

At this period, cast steel wire was being drawn at the Hathersage works of Robert Cocker, with specific mention of clock springs. Needle making appears to have been introduced - along with a few experienced workers - from the Studley, Worcestershire area. Records from Redditch show that their needle makers were obtaining wire from Hathersage by at least 1790. In 1798 one of the Hathersage suppliers was Thomas Cocker.

Samuel Cocker, who had been apprenticed to a Manchester needle maker, set up in the trade at Hathersage in 1810. He possibly held an additional interest in Barnfield Mill on the Hood Brook, sharing the premises with Robert Cook, a wire drawer who moved from Studley in 1811 and within 10 years was operating as Robert Cook & Co. of Barnfield Works. Cook produced cast steel wire, needles, gill pins, etc., and Barnfield was one of only three firms worldwide to manufacture hackle pins for combing wool and raising the nap on cloth. Fifty years after arriving in Hathersage, Robert Cook had 100 employees including 20 children. One nine-year-old girl told the Children's Employment Commission of 1862 that she was at work shaping umbrella ribs from 6 am to 7 pm. One 11-year-old boy said that he sometimes worked a 15-hour day.

The name of Henry Cocker is associated with Dale Mill on the Dale Brook, which he took over around 1824, when a second storey was added and the manufacture of brass buttons was abandoned in favour of wire drawing for the production of steel pins and needles. Henry Cocker was already producing these in workshops across the road from Dale Mill, the present Eastwood Cottages. A tunnel between the mill and the workshop may have been used for wire drawing.

Gramophones, bicycles and umbrellas

A mill later known as Victoria Works was in the hands of Tobias Child, who from the 1830s produced, amongst other things, hackle and gill pins for the textile industries. John Stead, a 'pin manufacturer', was here at the beginning of the 20th century. He also made gramophone needles.

Atlas Works, near the confluence of the Hood and Dale Brooks, was another wire drawing mill, operated between the 1840s and 1880s by the Cocker family, perhaps the first mill in Hathersage to change from water to steam power. Output from Atlas Works included bicycle spokes and umbrella frames, this latter having a firm local connection. The invention of the world's first successful collapsible umbrella frame is attributed to Bradwell-born Samuel Fox, though credit should mainly go to

Joseph Hayward, one of Fox's employees at the mighty Stocksbridge Steel Works. En route to fame and fortune, young Fox was apprenticed to Samuel Cocker and Sons in 1831 and initially worked as a wire drawer in Hathersage.

Water power for the Hathersage 'needle mills' was supplied by the Hood and Dale Brooks, with steam engines introduced from 1841. By the following decade, however, the needle industry was in general decline, and the factory of Samuel Cocker & Sons closed in 1852/3.

Robert Cook & Co. remained in business until the early 20th century, since which time the factory buildings have met various fates. The Atlas Works was demolished in 1907 after several years lying idle, while Victoria Works, which had moved into millstone production, closed down after the steam boiler blew up in 1910. Barnfield and Dale Mill chimneys are still standing, the factory buildings converted to residential and commercial use.

PORCELAIN AND POTWORKS

Any item made from baked clay is a form of pottery, whether as heavy as paving stones or as delicate and fragile as translucent porcelain. The potter's art has been practised by nearly every race since before the dawn of history, and in most corners of the world. Vital to the advance of civilisation, it depended on only two simple basics: ample supplies of clay, and fuel for firing (baking).

The Chinese claim that pottery manufacture was discovered around 2,700 BC by Emperor Hwang Tsi, who taught it to his people. This precious gift earned him a place amongst the Gods. But according to Greek myth, the world's first potter was Keramos (hence the word ceramic), son of the God Dionysus and Ariadne, daughter of King Minos of Crete.

Prehistoric production was known across Europe, and ancient vessels of burnt clay have been found in the Peak. They are particularly associated with the Bronze Age 'Beaker People', so named from the clay beakers found in their burial cairns, especially on Stanton Moor.

Coarser types of pottery are generally described as earthenware. Many kinds of clay can be used to produce earthenware, burning reddish or brownish in colour and always opaque. Once cleaned and purified, clay is shaped into vessels either by 'throwing' on a wheel or by moulding. After being fired in a kiln, the vessel may require glazing to prevent porosity. The glazing on Roman pots found in kilns at Derby racecourse contains lead, probably mined in the Peak.

Commercial production of English pottery really got under way after John Dwight of Fulham discovered the secret of manufacturing salt-glaze stoneware in 1671. The raw material, a highly siliceous clay, was fired at extremely high temperatures and the glaze was produced by throwing common salt into the kiln during firing. With the expiry of Dwight's patent in 1698, numerous salt-glaze potworks sprang up and the Peak was well served by several on its outskirts. A manufactory was established at Crich by brothers John and George Dodd, later joined by a third brother, Richard, a mug maker. All three became Burgesses of the City of Nottingham.

Other manufacturers set up at Chesterfield, Alfreton, Belper and Derby. Brown stoneware was common to them all, used for a vast array of everyday kitchenware such as cooking pots and storage jars, teapots, jugs, water filters and jelly moulds.

Porcelain, by contrast, was too expensive to be found in ordinary homes. The secret of its raw material - kaolin, a fine white clay - was not discovered in Europe until 1701, whereas the Chinese had been making porcelain for well over 1,000 years. One 10th-century Chinese emperor had demanded teacups "as blue as the sky, as clear as a mirror, as thin as paper, as resonant as a musical bell." The secret of this translucency was guarded very jealously. When exquisite Chinese porcelain was brought back to Europe by returning Crusaders, it was worth more than its weight in gold.

Wirksworth China

The first true European porcelain was made in Germany in the early 18th century. Then around 1755 'china clay' was found in Cornwall and porcelain was soon being produced at Plymouth and further afield. Suitable clays were eagerly sought after and although the geology of the Peak made it an unlikely source, Pilkington provides the following reference: "porcelain clay of a most delicate white colour and a very fine texture [is got] from a lead mine at Brassington ... what is gotten at present is sent to the potteries in Staffordshire. Also At Newhaven a very fine potters-clay may be had."

The Brassington source may have prompted the establishment of a china works that operated in Wirksworth from about 1772 until 1777. Recent research has pieced together the history of this single example of china manufacture in the Peak. Production came into being through the partnership of Sir Thomas Burdett of Foremark, the Hurts of Alderwasley, Mr Julius Caesar Robiglio and the Gells of the Gatehouse and Hopton. The new venture was set up in the grounds of Holland Manor House in Wirksworth, owned by Philip Gell.

Surviving documents indicate a wide variety of wares: bowls, cream jugs, teapots, sauce-boats, perfume jars, egg jars, plates, cups and saucers, pepper boxes and mustard pots. Ornamental items are also mentioned, as in an invoice from J.C. Stephan dated 18 August 1773:

"to Modelling - a flower Pott   1.17.6
Ditto - a Sfinks [sphinx] jar   3.3.0
Ditto - a Beaker   1.11.6
Ditto - two Dogs   0.11.6"
Other invoices refer to pedestals ornamented with rams' heads, and flower
jars with heads and horns, or women's faces. Some payments relate to
hand-painted decoration by J. Jackson and Mrs H. [possibly Hannah]
Smith.

John Charles Stephan was the son of Pierre Stephan, well known
for his figure modelling work at Derby. In May 1774, Stephan senior,
writing to Josiah Wedgwood, mentioned that he had a former connection
with the Wirksworth china factory. Now however, he was looking for "an
Opportunity of being Employ'd by persons of taste and merrits which I
hear is the Character of your Manufactory."

Wedgwood himself made an interesting entry in his Common
Place Book in 1775: "A China work - lately begun at Wirksworth - by Mr.
Gell of Hopton, who has lately made some use of a fine white Clay, found
near Brassington in Derbyshire, first in an estate of Mr. Haynes of
Ashburn, and afterwards in other adjoining lands ... It is found in low
lands, & black soil - about 12 yards and at other depths - in small lumps,
amongst inferior clays & other earths, and so uncertain, & in such small
quantities, as to be worth £10 per ton raising."

If the Wirksworth factory depended entirely upon this sparse
source, it is not surprising that production was short-lived. In May 1777,
an advertisement appeared in the Derby Mercury: "To be sold ... On
Wednesday the 18th day of this present month of May A great number of
elegant Plaister Moulds for Tureens, Plates, Dishes, Sauce boats in Sets,
Tea Services and Equipages with all other sorts requisite for a Manufactory
or Pot Work. A few very fine large Figures, Vases Urns Lamps exquisitely
moulded; Throwing Wheels, lathes and all other instruments necessary. A
quantity of Zaffer, Borax Red Lead, Lynn Sand Whiting Umber & Salts
with some fine fritt ready made. Enquire of Mrs. Dickins, the Three
Crowns, Wirksworth where a person will attend to these, the above article
& treat for the same."

Six months after the dispersal sale, Richard Arkwright of
Cromford took a lease on the buildings, warehouses and workshops
"heretofore used for the making and manufacture of China ware."

The site, still known as China Yard, is off St Mary's Gate in Wirksworth. Although pieces of 'Wirksworth china' have been handed down in local families, the absence of a manufacturer's mark makes it almost impossible to attribute them with certainty. Knowledge of styles and patterns remains elusive. Fragments found on the site have largely been lost but a small number were presented to the Victoria and Albert Museum in 1938. Wirksworth Heritage Centre has a display relating to the china factory and is fortunate in having a cup and saucer, also a hand-written bill.

ROPE MAKERS

Until comparatively recently, and within living memory, many Peak villages had a resident rope maker. Their craft was ages old but their equipment was simple and owed little to progress. The origins of rope and cord making go back thousands of years and we know that reeds, rushes and roots, as well as animal hair and strips of hide have all been twisted to make cord. The Egyptians learned to make strong ropes out of papyrus, the aquatic plant which also gave them paper.

The most useful materials available to later rope makers were hemp and flax. Real hemp was grown in great quantities in Italy, Russia and the USA. Strong and workable, it was much used for ships' rigging. The so-called Manila hemp did long service, though it was not really hemp at all, but the fibre of a wild banana plant native to the Philippines. Sisal was another important material, obtained from the leaves of a cactus-like plant native to Mexico, but later grown in large plantations in Java and East Africa. Sisal twine was rough, neither very pliable nor hard-wearing, but cheap enough to be almost disposable. This made it an ideal single-use binder twine for agricultural use.

All rope starts out as bundles of fibres, twisted into threads and strands then into string or twine. Thick string is called cord. Rope is made by twisting a number of strings or cords around one another in such a way that they will not unravel. The traditional rope maker began work by walking backwards from his spinning wheel with a bundle of loose fibres attached to his waist, spinning them into a cord as he went. In this manner ropeworkers went up and down their 'ropewalk' hundreds of times a day, many working in the open air but some inside long, low-roofed buildings.

A typical one-man business operated at Tansley until about 60 years ago, with John Barber supplying local needs all his working life, from plough lines, cart ropes and rope halters to clothes lines and skipping ropes. Although he had a wooden shed at the top of Green Lane, Mr Barber was usually to be found working outside, unrestricted by walls.

Ropewalk sites in many other villages are also on record. Bakewell boasted two: one near Endcliffe Quarry and another (Matleys) beside the present A6 on the south side of town. Four ropeworkers were listed at Bakewell in the early 1800s. A ropewalk on the Meadows at Wirksworth was active until at least 1833. The industry also ended at Monyash in the 19th century, the ropewalk being on the west side of the lane leading north from Cross Lanes. The site of a ropewalk at Winster is identifiable in the shape of a long narrow field almost opposite the old ore house at the top of Bonsall Lane. A dilapidated narrow enclosure at Uppertown, Bonsall, is where John Loxley spun hemp rope in the 1800s. A rope or hessian works is said to have been run by two brothers inside the extensive cellars of Taddington Hall, one brother manufacturing the goods and the other acting as a travelling salesman.

Signs of life

The oldest link with rope making in the Peak is kept alive on the historic ropewalks of Peak Cavern at Castleton. The vast mouth of the cavern has been associated with the industry for over five centuries. Tradition has it that the Duke of Devonshire, as lessee under the Duchy of Lancaster, owner of Peak Cavern, allowed rope makers to occupy the cavern rent-free "whilst ever there was a master or his apprentice working there."

This was a valuable concession. Not only did the rope makers work in this gloomy, sunless place, they lived here too - up to 40 families in the early 19th century. Two rows of cottages "built of stone or clay ... and thatched like little styes" stood against the walls - the soot from their chimneys can still be seen. There were also stables, an inn and three small shops. The last of the buildings was pulled down some time before 1870, though in 1935 an item in the *High Peak News* referred to Mrs Hannah Drinkwater, nee Hadfield, born on the Peak Cavern Walk around 1864.

Each ropewalk occupied one of a flight of terraces cut into the cavern floor and operated by one family or 'firm'. Ropeworkers commonly worked in pairs, often father and son, sometimes mother and daughter. This underground industry became one of the Peak's earliest tourist attractions and achieved wide fame through the writings of travellers. Around 1682, Charles Cotton wrote in *Wonders of the Peake*:

"Now to the Cave we come, wherein is found
A new strange thing, a village under Ground;
Houses and Barns for Men and Beasts Behoof,
With Walls distinct, under one solid Roof."

And exactly 100 years later, from Moritz's *Travels*: "I perceived to the right, in the hollow of the Cavern, a whole subterranean village, where the inhabitants, on account of it being Sunday, were resting from their work, and with happy and cheerful looks were sitting at the doors of their huts along with their children." In that same year William Bray describes how two old women, Betty Blowitt and Sal Waugh, would emerge from their houses to beg from visitors. Younger residents had a useful sideline as guides, speedily appearing with a lantern or candles to conduct visitors on a tour of the extensive cavern.

Females began to learn their craft at an early age, starting with light work. A visitor of around 1812 describes how "on one side were the young girls belonging to the inkle manufactory, turning their wheels, winding thread, and amusing their companies with cheerful songs; whilst the rope makers opposite to them were spinning cords and twisting cables, forming them into coils."

Inkle was flax, plaited into a thin braid and widely used as candle wick. Flax, jute and cotton all found a use in Peak Cavern, with Italian hemp the major raw material by the mid-19th century. Over the generations, Castleton rope makers adapted to the changing demands of agriculture and industry, from the needs of lead mines and breweries to tow ropes for barges, washing lines, window sashes, bell ropes - and, it is said, the occasional hangman's rope.

Castleton Garland

Family links appear in parish records which name residents of 'Peakes Hole', with an occasional note that one or the other was a twine spinner. Families named Hall, Whittingham, Dakin, Walker, Eyre and Hadfield were all engaged in this trade. The last rope maker, Herbert Marrison, retired in 1975 aged 91. He had worked in Peak Cavern since the age of 12, following his father, Joseph, and grandfather, Abraham, into 'the firm'. One of the highlights of his career was completing an order from a north-east shipping company for an 8-mile length of string, which, when checked by the pernickety customer, had a 7-yard 'bonus'. Until the end of his working life Bert Marrison turned out a steady supply of clothes lines; he personally maintained the custom of providing one for every new bride in Castleton.

Another old custom depended on Peak Cavern rope makers. Castleton Museum has a balance sheet for the 1926 Garland ceremony, showing the expenditure of one shilling (5p) for a maypole rope purchased from Joseph Marrison. He, and later his son, upheld the long-standing tradition of producing two other essential items for the Castleton Garland: string to tie bunches of flowers to the Garland and rope to haul it onto the church tower.

In line with Bert Marrison's last wishes, his ashes were laid to rest inside Peak Cavern. His old skills are kept alive by part-time rope makers with an interest in the craft, using contraptions all more than a century old.

A ropewalk

SILK INDUSTRIES

An indication of the antiquity of breeding silk worms, or sericulture, lies in a Chinese story set about 4,600 years ago, telling how the wife of Emperor Huang Ti found a way to unravel the cocoons of silk worms. Even though it took 1,200 threads laid side by side to cover a single inch (2.5cm), and 1,000 cocoons to make just one gown, there were people in China with patience enough to spin the threads into cloth. The Empress, it is said, was made a goddess for giving silk to the world.

Chinese silk began to find its way into other lands and was highly prized, but the method of manufacture was kept secret, and silk remained a rare and costly luxury for hundreds of years. Under Chinese law, the death penalty awaited anyone who took either silk worms or eggs out of the country, or even the mulberry seeds on which silk worms fed. Outsiders knew so little that they thought silk was a crop.

In time the secret leaked out, and by at least the 15th century raw silk was being imported into England from Italy and France. The Far East remained the chief source, since the breeding of silkworms and the handling of cocoons was only viable where there was an abundance of cheap labour. In the sense that the silkworm has already spun its threads, silk does not need to be spun like cotton or wool. However, the gossamer-like threads have to be combined into larger strands for weaving into fabric.

Attempts at breeding silkworms in England were unsuccessful. Even the great naturalist Sir Joseph Banks had no luck, although the mulberry tree which he planted in his garden at Ashover still survives.

The various preparatory processes of throwing, twisting, winding and dyeing silk thread gradually became well established. By the late 1600s, Macclesfield throwsters were supplying high quality thread to the silk weavers of Spitalfields in London, who had settled and set up their looms here after fleeing religious persecution in France.

In 1702 Thomas Cotchett set up silk throwing machinery in a mill on the Derwent in Derby. By 1789 Derby had 12 mills, while Macclesfield had become the country's major silk weaving centre. During the Napoleonic wars Macclesfield benefited enormously from a nationwide ban on the import of French silk.

Fine silk demanded the highest quality thread. Inferior grades, known as waste, were perfectly adequate for such items as ribbon, hat bands, fringes, sewing thread, stockings and knee garters, all produced by home workers around Macclesfield and Leek. After the construction of a branch of the Caldon Canal in the 1790s, the number of silk workers centred on Leek grew to more than 3,000. Largely working from their own homes, they specialised in gowns, shawls, haberdashery and kerchiefs. Silk dyeing was established in the town in the early 19th century.

Into the Peak

From Macclesfield and Leek it was no great distance to villages on the Staffordshire moorlands. A silk mill existed on the River Dane at Gradbach as early as 1640, while 19th-century enterprise led to the establishment of a small industrial village around Gradbach Mill, Quarnford. This mill was operated in the 1860s by Bowden Bower Dakeyn, who also worked Dane Bridge silk mill near Wincle. Gradbach ceased production in the 1870s and the workers' cottages have since been demolished.

Production had already ended at Gin Clough Mill, Rainow, where handlooms were worked in many homes for over a century. Hollinsclough told a similar story; in the latter half of the 18th century, almost 50 households supplemented their income by weaving small articles of Macclesfield silk. Packhorses crossing Axe Edge delivered the thread to Hollinsclough and took back finished work to the merchants of Macclesfield. In the late 1800s, one solitary, very old silk weaver was still at work in a shed near her cottage on the edge of Hollinsclough Moor.

During the 18th and 19th centuries, a cottage industry thrived at Middleton by Youlgreave, where women wove silk and cotton lace. (see Lace Making)

A major factor leading to the demise of home weaving was the abolition in 1824 of high import duties on imported raw silk. This was intended to concentrate resources on throwing rather than weaving, with the result that only looms powered by water or steam remained truly viable.

The large Crag Mills at Wildboarclough were purpose-built silk mills with machinery installed by James Brindley. A small silk mill stood on the sheepwash at Peak Forest, and another was recorded at the bottom of Water Lane, Bradwell in 1800. Others stood at Alstonefield, where 64 silk workers were employed in 1838, and at Upper Hulme on the River Churnet, which converted to silk dyeing in 1869.

Wirksworth Heritage Centre is housed in the old Crown Yard silk and velvet mill in the market place. (see Velvet & Fustian Cutters) This business was established in the late 1840s by Samuel Evans, husband of Elizabeth, the aunt of novelist George Eliot. The mill flourished and Samuel Evans junior followed his father into the business. He appears on the 1851 census as 'draper and silk manufacturer' and is known to have employed nearly 30 workers. A general depression closed the mill around 1878.

Eyam and Tideswell

Meanwhile, Eyam and Tideswell had become active silk weaving centres, with three workshops operating at Eyam in 1857. Yarn was fetched on foot from Tideswell, where an agency had been set up as a collection point by dealers from Macclesfield. Finished goods included brightly-coloured scarves and handkerchiefs for export in large quantities to Africa. A silk workshop at the west end of Eyam, later used as a shoe factory, belonged to Ralph Wain who, after many years of trying, developed a process for reproducing designs on both sides of silk fabric. Wain, an illiterate semi-recluse, was persuaded to sell his valuable invention to the Macclesfield firm supplying his silk.

Handloom silk weaving was introduced to Tideswell as a cottage industry in the early 19th century. Again the silk came from Macclesfield and the trade continued until about 1900. Production at the old silk mills of Derby had already ended, whereas Paradise Mill at Macclesfield continued as a working silk mill until 1981. It is now a museum open to visitors.

THE STAY WORKS

The heartfelt expression, "Ooh! I'll have to loosen my stays" has almost passed out of use. It tended to issue from the lips of an anguished lady of mature years whose face, if not her figure, certainly looked better for the loosening, for stays was another name for a corset. To be precise, stays were the strips of steel or bone (properly called busks), sewn into the corset to keep it rigid.

Corset making in the Peak is represented by Ashbourne, where references to the Stay Works were once as familiar as the factory's proper name, Richard Cooper & Co. This enterprise was born in 1855 when Richard Cooper and Charles Smith set on a handful of women to make corsets. Five years later, now with 25 operatives, production was moved to larger premises, followed by further expansion into a newly-built factory in 1864. The firm flourished, passing into the hands of Cooper's son, William Hill Cooper, to become a Private Limited Company in 1905 with over 500 employees. Factory accommodation was added to the already extensive site, but continuing growth created more jobs than could easily be filled in Ashbourne. Branch factories were opened at Uttoxeter and Derby; such was the demand that in 1910 each doubled its capacity.

Shortly faced with the restrictions of wartime, the firm added knitted goods to its range, enjoying steady progress until the outbreak of the Second World War. Production of underclothing for the armed services had to be curtailed when a substantial part of the Ashbourne factory was taken over by Rolls-Royce, while the branch factories were commandeered by the Ministry of Food and the Ministry of Works. Fortunately, the Board of Trade did not deem the corset to be a luxury garment, so allocations of precious cloth and materials allowed continued and significant manufacture at Ashbourne. In a gradual move away from supplying retailers under their own brand names, Cooper's mainly marketed their goods under the Excelsior label, registered back in 1883.

After the lean years of the 1940s, the home and export markets began to boom and in 1950, to overcome severe labour shortages in and around Ashbourne, Cooper's began to provide electric sewing machines free of charge for women to work at home. Production opened up at Buxton in 1953, while a new factory was built to trade as Knitted Garments Ltd alongside the main Ashbourne corset factory.

'A funny shape'

Records dating from the firm's inception are deposited with Derbyshire Record Office in Matlock, providing much of interest to the social historian. One file of 50-year-old letters brings a touch of light relief to the staid ledgers and advertising material, and surely must have brought a smile to the staff of the Personal Service Bureau - perhaps the reason for saving them. Most of the correspondence is in fact from men, often enclosing an order as a surprise gift for "my lady". But one Midlands man suggests some advertising slogans as he confesses that "I have always had a liking for corsets (I don't really know why)." One gentleman, enquiring about a serviceable corset for his 12-stone (76-kg) "Little Ray of Sunshine", gives her dimensions as height 5ft 1inch (155cm), chest 42 inches (107cm), hips 43 inches (109cm).

A flurry of enquiries from Africa requests free illustrated sales catalogues as mentioned in *Photoplay*! A Nigerian schoolboy seems confused as to what he can order, his needs being "mostly that of Silvikrin for my dried hair ... please consider me and have pity on my poor nerves." Two men serving with the Royal Signals at Benghazi make a plea for penfriends of the opposite sex, while a man from the Gold Coast offers to send a monkey's skin in return for books and pictures. An 11-year-old schoolboy from Sekondi - writing on behalf of himself and three younger brothers - requests photographs, promising to send one of himself in exchange.

A worn-out pair of stays apparently accompanied a letter from a Staffordshire lady, asking whether another pair could be made to the same style as "I am a funny shape." A younger correspondent, obviously aspiring to the egg-timer look, enquires whether Cooper's can provide (on approval) a corset capable of reducing her 21 inch (53cm) waist by 4/5 inches (10-13cm). In reply a personal adviser informs madam that the smallest available size is 23 inches (58cm), adding archly: "Anyway, I should think a 21 inch waist was quite small enough!"

The firm deigned to accept a special 20 inch (50cm) order from a St Albans draper who stated that his customer, when quite young, had been made to wear this particular style of corset by her mother. Although she now had a grown-up family of her own, the daughter was still able to squeeze herself into a 20 inch corset.

The wife of a London gentleman confides that although he has kept his figure "in parts", he might consider wearing a lady's corset. It would need to be a strong, high-waisted garment since "the upper part of his diaphragm has become overdeveloped and somewhat protruding ... yet through his constant efforts to see that he wears an abdominal belt his waist is exactly the same as 10 years ago."

The file ends with just one letter of complaint, about a bra "made all wrong ... a waste of good money." Although there is no mention of feather trimmings, the dissatisfied customer offers the unwittingly humorous comment that she has "never seen anything quite so poultry."

Richard Cooper and Company was taken over by a national conglomerate in the 1970s and production at Cooper's Mill ceased around 1980. Its successor in Ashbourne is the firm of Chiltex, where traditional corsetry and modern lingerie are still made today.

THE SWEET SMELL OF SUCCESS AT CRESSBROOK

But for the commercial endeavours of a man named John Baker, the village of Cressbrook would almost certainly have remained Grassbrook. In his younger days Baker and his partner, John Gardom, owned Litton 'frame knittery', a small stocking factory close to Litton church. In due course the two men went their separate ways; Baker set up businesses in Manchester and Liverpool while Gardom went on to build Calver Mill.

In the meantime, Baker expanded his local interests by virtue of the Litton Enclosures of 1763. The enclosures resulted in the formation of two large estates bordering on the River Wye. One estate comprised land from Miller's Dale to Water-cum-Jolly and was allotted to Lord Scarsdale, as Lord of the Manor; the other, consisting of woodland known as Litton Frith, fell to John Baker, gentleman.

Litton Frith extended from Water-cum-Jolly to the junction of the Cress Brook and the Wye. The brook ran through a sheltered but badly overgrown valley, and Baker put clearance work in hand. With the brook flowing clearly once more, he began cultivating beds of watercress on a commercial basis. Cress harvests were so plentiful that the old place-name of Grassbrook gradually gave way to Cressbrook.

Baker also had the hillsides cleared of undergrowth and set with filbert and fruit trees, with the gentler slopes towards the river reserved for large beds of lavender and peppermint, the first stage in his next venture. This saw the erection of a distillery to extract the plants' pungent essences. Baker built himself a fine house in this pretty spot by the Wye. Three storeys high, it was constructed beneath a "beautiful Concave Rock, forming a complete Roof." There is no longer any such house but a rock by the mill dam suggests where it may have stood. Unfortunately the distillery burned down in 1788 and was not replaced. Apart from the name Cressbrook, all traces of John Baker's enterprise have disappeared, except perhaps for some holes in the rocks behind Cressbrook Mill, where his aromatic plants were supposedly hung to dry.

TANNERS AND LEATHERWORKERS

The history of curing animal skins is too old to guess at; leather has been found with prehistoric remains and in Egyptian tombs. Recent by comparison, the oldest surviving examples of leather in the Peak are remnants of footwear dating from the Roman occupation, displayed in Buxton Museum.

Skins can be made resistant to bacteriological decay by steeping them in tannin. Oak bark was formerly the primary source of tannin, so the tanning process was common to country areas, convenient too for supplies of cattle hides. A town-based tanner was likely to buy his hides from local butchers or abattoirs.

The following advertisement is taken from the *Derby Mercury*: "Bark Peelers Wanted - To peel this season 1793 a large quantity of oak coppice timber at Bradley near Ashbourne. As the timber stands in five coppices any person may be treated with to peel any one lot or the whole by applying to Mr Buxton, Tanner, Ashbourne, or Mr Fearn, Timber Merchant, Bradley."

A later advertisement refers to a forthcoming auction, on 12 October 1796, of a tanyard at Wirksworth together with a croft of about an acre-and-a-half, the property of Joseph Sattersfield. Established some 50 years and with a plentiful supply of water in a neighbourhood well stocked with oak timber, the business comprised "43 Pitts, 44 Handlers, 6 lime pitts, 3 drying rooms and 2 excellent bark mills."

In the same year, *Derby Mercury* printed an announcement from the Company of Tanners which quoted extracts from Acts of Parliament passed under James I in relation to the illegal stripping of oak bark: "That no person or persons shall regrate, ingress, or get into their hands by buying, contracting, or promise-taking, any Oaken Bark, before it be stripped or after, to the intent to sell the same again, upon pain of forfeiture of all such Bark, so by him or them regrated, ingrossed, or bought contrary to the true meaning of this branch, or the full value thereof."

Leather was essential to the two main trades of footwear (see Boot and Shoemakers) and saddlery. A hundred years ago, saddlers and harness makers were in business all around the Peak, turning out saddles, heavy padded collars for farm horses, and smaller items from blinkers to reins. Mills and factories needed machinery-belting and strapping, while men employed in heavy work bought leather breeches and protective boots. The railway created a market for hoods to link coaches together, upholstery and window straps for passenger carriages and hosepipes for watering engines.

Tanning and currying

All leather products depend in the first place on the skills of the tanner. A skinyard, or tanyard, operating by a stream used to be a familiar sight - and smell. An advertisement of 1800 reads: "Mr Philip Dawson and Mr Henry Dale have entered into partnership to carry on the business of tanning (late the property and in the occupation of Mr Job Holbrook in Compton in Ashbourne). Notice is hereby given that anyone who may have raw Hides, Skins, Kips, etc., to dispose of or any butcher whose slaughters are not engaged shall have the best Market Price and ready money for same."

Ox hides were favoured for toughness, with cow and bull similarly suited to hard wear, while heifer produced a more supple leather. The softest leather came from calf skin, kid skin and other young animals - the 'kips' referred to above.

All hides were treated in the same way. The initial salting-down process was followed by a thorough soaking in water to remove the salt and dirt, hence the need for proximity to ample supplies of running water. The hides were next laid in lime pits - and lime was readily available in the Peak - to loosen the hair and soften the skin fibres. This made it easy to scrape off the hair and remaining flesh, the latter to be sold to soap and glue manufacturers, then all traces of lime were removed by agitating the hides in water containing an enzymatic 'bate'. Dog dung often provided the necessary enzymes before the commercial production of bate.

The hides were next passed through pits of tanning liquid of increasing strength, then left to soak for about six weeks in the strongest solution before being very slowly and carefully dried under cover. Lastly they were handed over to be dressed and, if necessary, dyed by the currier, a skilled craftsman often in business on his own account. The currying process involved impregnating the leather with grease to leave it soft and supple, chiefly using 'dubbin', a mix of equal parts of cod liver oil and beef tallow. Heavy leathers were usually dipped in a tank of molten grease, commonly paraffin wax.

Leather was a major export and a tanner could be quite a wealthy member of the community. On the domestic front he was essential to the boot and shoemakers found in any village of moderate size. This interdependence is noticed in trade directories. In the 1830s, for example, a Wirksworth tanner and a leather dresser at New Bridge both enjoyed regular trade with three saddler/harness makers in Wirksworth and Cromford. Bakewell and Baslow each supported a tanner and two saddlers. A tanner/currier listed at Grindleford Bridge probably occupied the large premises on Goatscliffe Brook, partly taken over by Grindleford Laundry in 1913. The row of houses at the bottom of the hill approaching Grindleford from the Calver direction were built over the tanyard and originally named Tanyard Cottages, now Goatscliffe Cottages.

Grindleford tannery would have been a major source of leather for many boot and shoemakers. In the 1830s, in addition to those at Hathersage, Eyam and Stoney Middleton, others were to be found in Tideswell, Peak Forest and Calver. Three were listed at Hope and three at Bradwell which, until the end of the 19th century, also had a tannery behind the old sawmill on Bradwell Brook.

Edale Mill on the River Noe was a tannery prior to its conversion to a cotton mill. A nearby house provided accommodation for the tannery workers; nicknamed Skinner's Hall, the name has stuck.

The Staffordshire side of the Peak had leatherworks at Winkhill and Ecton. Saddlery was a speciality of Longnor, where quarrymen's leather boots were produced within living memory. The demand for tough footwear in lead mining and quarrying areas was reflected in local businesses, as at Winster, which in 1835 supported two leather dealers and seven boot/shoemakers.

A rare skill is represented in Bakewell Old House Museum in the form of ornamental leather-work depicting fruit and flowers - examples of a former cottage industry tentatively attributed to Stanton in Peak. This painstaking and attractive craft appears to have been unique as far as the Peak is concerned and surviving pieces are extremely rare.

TAPES AND NARROW FABRICS

In the latter years of the 19th century, the weekly output of 230 employees at Speedwell and Haarlem Mills in Wirksworth equalled the circumference of the Earth. These workers were producing tape, a description applied to a wide range of narrow fabrics, from boot laces to ferrets (stout cotton or silk tapes) and smallwares (haberdashery). The medieval word 'taeppe' described any narrow cloth used for any conceivable purpose.

Demand for tape was well established long before commercial manufacture began in Derby in the early 19th century. Ashbourne and Wirksworth followed the Derby mills into production, and together these three towns were to form the nucleus of the largest tape producing centre in the world.

A small number of outlying manufacturers included John Hackett, listed in 1821 as a tape maker in the Matlock area, probably at Tansley, where Thomas Hackett was later producing tape. In 1822/3 a dam was constructed on the River Bradford to work the 9-ton water wheel of a tape and bobbin mill in Middleton Dale. (see Bobbin Mills) In 1829 there was mention of Tatlow and Fletcher's smallware factory by the first dam in Middleton Dale, though by 1846 the building stood unoccupied. It later served other uses and the large overshot wheel was eventually put to work pumping water for the village water supply.

Tape making flourished best at Wirksworth. Haarlem Mill, a cotton mill formerly worked in conjunction with Arkwright's Cromford Mills but paralysed by the cotton depression, was converted to tape weaving by 1815. Willow Bath tape mill dates from the same period, while the steam-powered Speedwell Mill, a former hat factory, was converted to tape manufacture by Joseph Wheatcroft in 1844. In 1879 the Wheatcroft firm acquired the steam and water-powered Haarlem Mill. They subsequently set up their own bleachworks and dye yard at Wash Green in Wirksworth, eliminating the expense of sending material to Matlock for bleaching.

In 1883 John Bowmer and Sons began tape making at Wirksworth's Providence Mill, later known as Gorsey Bank Mill. Bowmers would later make the proud boast that they had manufactured the fuse-binding tape of every Mills Bomb, a type of grenade, used in the First World War. The firm built a new mill at Water Lane in 1961 and nine years later merged with M. Bond and Company of Ashbourne to become Bowmer-Bond Narrow Fabrics, operating at Hanging Bridge Mills on the

River Dove in Ashbourne. Bonds could trace their tape making origins to Alrewas in 1795, moving to Ashbourne in 1866.

Such are the firms responsible for producing immeasurable quantities of the notorious red tape beloved of bureaucrats everywhere.

Ahead of its time

Nineteenth-century fashion kept domestic demands high too, whether ribbons, laces, trimmings, or strong bindings for the huge market in corsets. (see The Stay Works) Taking Messrs Lowe & Scholes of Tansley as an example, a typical late 19th-century range of goods included corset binding, India tape, carpet binding, skirt beltings and venetian blind webbing. Lowe & Scholes operated two large four-storey mills powered by five mill dams and their promotional material announced that the machinery was "attended to by a small army of workers, all experienced skilled hands, smart, intelligent and industrious." Many employees started young; by the time tape weaver Joseph Ball retired in the summer of 1897, aged 77, he had worked at Tansley tape mills for 70 years.

In 1899 a revolutionary invention called the Poyser Tape Loom made the news. The ingenious Mr John Poyser of Bolehill, Wirksworth was in the process of setting up his prototype at the old Malt House on Steeple Grange. This 'tape or ribbon loom' was the subject of a lecture at the Yorkshire College by Professor Beaumont, who declared that the inventor had achieved what 99 out of 100 persons would say was the 'Utopia of a dreamer', but had succeeded so remarkably that he was entitled to be ranked amongst the foremost textile inventors. The Professor expected the loom to be "an epoch-making one in the textile world." Unfortunately his optimism was misplaced, for the equipment was so far ahead of its time that existing yarn technology could not match the speed of the shuttles. The only firm that entirely installed the Poyser Loom went into liquidation. Yet its revolutionary speed foreshadowed later technical advances, although shuttles were ultimately made obsolete by the introduction of needle looms.

Bowmer-Bond of Ashbourne is now sole survivor of the old tape makers of the Peak. The factory still uses the traditional mainstay, cotton, but on a vastly smaller scale than modern materials such as PVC and polypropylene webbings, produced for specialist needs in the transport industry and such diverse items as luggage and camera straps, equestrian and mountaineering equipment.

THATCHING

Within a single lifetime, the skills of the thatcher, or thacker, have been almost phased out of existence in the Peak, with few left to practise a craft unbroken from prehistoric times.

The few people who now live in thatched houses will attest that they are warmer in winter and cooler in summer than hard-roofed dwellings. Unfortunately, thatch is also favoured for wasps' and bees' nests and tales are told of homes burned down through attempts to smoke out resident insects. That aside, thatch was indeed a fire hazard in built-up areas, where sparks and flames could leap from roof to roof. That risk was probably in the minds of the bailiffs and burgesses of Derby when, in 1574, they granted a lease on a property on condition that the incoming tenant "new build the same and cover with tyle."

It was eventually discovered that thatch could be fireproofed using a mixture of alum and lime, a cost offset into the 20th century by a reduction in fire insurance premiums.

One early type of thatch utilised wheat stubble, the short straw left behind when the corn was cut. It was sometimes applied to roofs in alternate layers between wet clay, or road sweepings mixed with lime. Stubble thatch was cheap, but lasted for less than 20 years, whereas wheat straw, sedges, rushes, flags and reeds gave a far longer life. Rye had a good reputation for the length and strength of its straw, and Norfolk reed is still used for superior durability. The most commonly used materials in the Peak were wheat straw and rush. The essential long stalks of straw were readily available in the days when it was stooked in the field after harvest - today's baled straw would be useless to the thatcher. He bought direct from the farmer, who in turn was a good customer; thatch gave excellent insulation to his stock buildings.

A rush thatch lasted longer than straw and was likely to be used if it grew locally. At Castleton we find Rushup Edge, which also provided rushes for the annual rush bearing ceremony in Peak Forest church, while the place names Rushton Spencer and Rushton James lie to the west of the Peak District National Park.

Farmers on the Staffordshire moorlands made detachable rush roofs to protect hayricks left out in the fields. The thatch was anchored down with stakes and ropes against the winter weather, but could be lifted off to get at the hay as needed.

Straw finials

Large scale thatching has always been left to the expert. Preparations begin by soaking the straw in water to make it pliable. It is then straightened and gathered into thick, heavy bundles called yealms (Old English for a handful), bound with either twine or a straw bond. Work on the roof begins by laying the yealms tightly side by side and overlapping, to be fixed in place with wooden pegs or spars, traditionally of hazel or willow. The completed thatch has an overhang to prevent rain from running straight off the roof and down the walls.

It is said that a well-thatched roof will last 80 to 100 years if the ridge is kept in good repair. Thatchers often top off the ridge with a trademark straw finial. In the 19th century, a Derbyshire roof might have been surmounted by cocks and hens, miniature sheaves of corn, chimneys, crosses and, in one instance, a little man with a gun at one end of the roof aiming towards a crow at the other end.

Thatch gradually began to be replaced by Welsh slate, or sometimes the heavy gritstone slate traditional to the Peak. Generally speaking, thatch continued to be seen longest on poorer, tenanted property, as low rents could not justify the cost of strengthening work needed for the change to slate.

Of the few remaining thatched properties around the Peak, one of the most photographed is the house called Thatch End at Nether End, Baslow. Another example is seen between Pilsley and Baslow, west of the road leading from Chatsworth. Idridgehay has a thatched house named South Sitch, dating from at least the early 17th century. Almost hidden from view is a thatched cottage near the Malt Shovel at Wirksworth. Another stands on Nottingham Road in Tansley, and a charming roadside cottage with a low thatched roof is found on the outskirts of Ashover. A cluster of thatched roofs survive at Osmaston, south-east of Ashbourne, adding a picturesque touch to Coronation Cottages, the village hall and several estate houses.

The Peak also has a connection with the thatched Revolution House at Old Whittington, near Chesterfield, where the 4th Earl, later 1st Duke, of Devonshire helped to hatch the plot behind the Glorious Revolution. The Revolution House is open to the public, admission free.

Traditional thatching

VELVET AND FUSTIAN CUTTERS

Soft and plush, velvet has always been favoured as one of the more luxurious fabrics. Manufacture used to be particularly labour intensive, making it far more expensive than coarser fabrics like wool and linen.

The early use of velvet was almost exclusively confined to robes for royalty and the wealthiest of the nobility, also for religious vestments. An inventory of 1295 refers to chasubles (sleeveless garments) of velvet at St Paul's in London. One of the oldest surviving examples of velvet in Britain is also related to religious ceremonial, being part of a 14th-century cape belonging to the College of Mount St Mary in Chesterfield.

Dyed in rich colours, velvet garments were worn on occasions of state, from coronations to funerals. Mary, Queen of Scots, made her final appearance in a gown of black satin and a petticoat of red velvet, worn to her execution in 1587. A few years later Bess of Hardwick, the wife of Mary's former gaoler, the Earl of Shrewsbury, spent some of her immense wealth on a litter to carry her back to Hardwick from London. Drawn by four horses, the litter was upholstered in velvet and had windows of gold parchment.

As velvet became less exclusive it was used to add an expensive touch to clothing; the supple 'collar velvet', for instance, was much in demand for gentlemen's overcoats.

Tideswell velveteen

True velvet is woven from silk with a short, smooth pile created by severing certain warp threads so that they stand erect. A fabric closely resembling true velvet is produced by using a foundation texture of either silk warp and cotton weft or entirely cotton. One such example, velveteen, is a variety of fustian, as are the more durable corduroy, moleskin and imperial sateen. These fabrics became affordable when duty on fustian was lifted in 1785.

Velvet was originally woven on handlooms and the depth of pile depended on the ratio of pile-warp threads to foundation-warp threads. During weaving, the pile-warp threads were raised to form a row of loops, called a 'shed', across the width of the fabric. Thin steel wires with a narrow groove on the upper surface were inserted through the shed to support the loops as they were cut open with a fine knife, the blade guided along the groove by a special frame. This produced close rows of uniform tufts - the pile.

Velvet cutting was not widely carried out in the Peak. From descriptions of the Rising Sun 'velvet' factory in Tideswell, it seems clear that the fabric produced was actually velveteen. This former cotton factory had changed to fustian and velvet cutting around 1890 and the business was for many years in the hands of John William Smith, employing some 30 women on piece work for about 15 shillings (75p) a week. By the 1920s his sons, John Wilfred and Arnold, were in charge.

The basic fustian was woven in Oldham and sent by rail to Miller's Dale station to await collection from Tideswell. When it reached the factory, the fustian, a thick unbleached material, was stiffened with lime and stretched taut on a frame ten yards (9 m) long. Women walked from one end of the frame to the other, cutting through the loops row by row with a keen blade made from a watch spring, sharpened to a fine point on a whetstone. It was said that during one day's work the women walked almost as far as Manchester. Finally, the pile was fluffed up with a wire brush and the 'velvet' was returned to Oldham to be dyed ready for sale.

A later velvet factory was established at Tideswell in a small former silk mill on Lower Terrace Road. Like the Rising Sun, it closed in 1933.

Wirksworth velvet

Wirksworth Heritage Centre occupies a former silk and velvet mill in Crown Yard, an alley just off the market place. (see Silk Industries) The mill was established by Samuel Evans and continued under his son, also Samuel, a cousin of the novelist George Eliot (whose real name was Mary Ann Evans). Few detailed records of the venture survive, but as silk was involved it is almost certain that true velvet was produced rather than velveteen. Work flourished from the late 1840s to 1870s, at one time employing nearly 30 workers. The property was mortgaged in 1868 when the occupants were Stephen Mason, druggist, and Messrs J. and T. Robinson of Sachaverel Street, Derby and Cheapside, London.

Ten years later a general depression closed the mill, throwing a number of people out of work. Pieces of fabric manufactured in the building are on display in Wirksworth Heritage Centre, where a rope still in place around one of the beams was probably used as leverage by a worker using foot treadle machines.

THE WOOL TRADES

The woollen industry, with all its many branches, has had a profound influence on life in the Peak. The natural landscape is well suited to large-scale sheep farming, which began long before open fields were enclosed within our distinctive dry-stone walls.

Vast medieval sheep farming granges were established by monastic houses on the limestone uplands, providing an enormous contribution to the country's woollen industry and immense profits to their religious orders. One early documentary source refers to the death in 1243 of 800 sheep at Bradbourne, a chapelry of Dunstable Priory. In 1295 the Priory, "due to the poverty of Bradbourne, granted to their brothers, the canons resident, their wool and all other profits except the tithes of Brassington for that year."

In 1280, Dieu la Cresse Abbey, near Leek, was described by a merchant of Florence as being his wool supplier, annually producing over three tons of wool. Nearby Wincle Grange, built a century later by the Cistercians, is thought to have been a collection point for wool awaiting export to the Continent. Cistercian monks also developed a 400-acre sheep farm at Roystone Grange, exporting wool to Europe and beyond. Although the Black Death halved the number of monks and lay brothers, the resulting labour shortages barely affected sheep farming. A fulling mill for cleansing and thickening woollen cloth was in use at Hartington as early as 1384. Sheep farming continued to expand and by 1500 England had three sheep to every human being.

The twin occupations of wool spinning and weaving formed one of the earliest and most enduring cottage industries, expanding rapidly in the High Peak from the early 1500s. Peakland wool and woollen goods were traded with centres in Yorkshire along a packhorse route to Halifax Gate, a traffic of sufficient importance in the early 18th century for Yorkshire wool merchants to contribute £10 towards repairing Leadmill Bridge at Hathersage.

A record of 1657 refers to Tenter Yard Croft at Hathersage. A tenter was a large wooden frame on which woollen cloth was stretched to dry, probably serving communal use. As an important needle making centre (see Pins and Needles), Hathersage also produced its own hackle pins for carding and combing wool. Worsted spinning, which produced a fine, smooth yarn from combed wool, took place at Litton and Tideswell until at least 1830. A Tideswell comb (woolcomber's) shop was pulled down for road widening in 1841.

The patron saint of wool combers is St Blasius or Blaze, a martyred Bishop who was tortured with iron combs. His festival was celebrated by mill workers in Bradford and other Yorkshire mill towns and similarly in the Peak. Wool workers around Tideswell held their annual revelries at a local inn, referred to in contemporary records by the name of its proprietor: "1795, Feb. 7, I was at B. Baker's from 6 o'clock to about 12, with Mr. F. Baker and his stockingers. They held Blaze today. Sam Slack was singing." And from 1799: "Feb.5, Shrove Tuesday, Mr. Francis Baker kept his Bishop Blaze today at his mother-in-law's, Molly Baker. I went to them about 4 o'clock and stay'd till betwixt 1 and 2 in the morning."

Other curious references are connected with an Act of Parliament passed in the reign of Charles II in an attempt to boost the depressed English woollen trade. An initial act of 1666 decreed that no person was to be buried in any material except woollen, a law reinforced with a second Act dictating that even the coffin was to be lined with nothing but sheep's wool. Typical of entries found in parish registers is the following from Darley Dale: "No corpse of any person (except those who shall die of the plague) shall be buried in any shift, sheet, shroud, or anything whatsoever made or mingled with any flax, hemp, silk, heir [hair], gold or silver, or in any stuff or thing other than what is made of sheep's wool, only upon pain of the forfeiture of £5."

Certificates were issued by the officiating clergyman, worded along the lines of: "Mary Wild maketh Oath that Edward Frost, of Wardlow, in the parish of Bakewell, and county of Derbe, lately decd., was not buried in any material but what was made of sheep's wool only. Swore before me, John Goddard. Curate of Wormhill. Testd., Mary Goddard, Strellay Moresby."

Parish registers contain many burial entries followed by the words 'buried in woollen', but some ladies simply would not be seen dead wearing wool and they left firm instructions otherwise. A fine of £5 was in any case a mere trifle to the executors of women like Mistress Temperance Gell of Hopton Hall, who in 1730 was buried in a linen shroud. The law was similarly observed on behalf of three women buried at Sheen in the late 17th century, while Longstone records refer to £5 paid by the relatives of an actress who had demanded to be buried in a satin shroud. The 'burial in woollen' act was already widely disregarded by the time it was repealed in 1815.

Mechanisation

Domestic spinning and hand-knitting of woollen stockings continued into the 19th century, both to keep the family in hose and to earn money. Travelling wool buyers, known as 'braggers', purchased raw wool from farmers and delivered it to home workers, returning to buy their finished work. Weaving was sometimes carried out communally, as at Holme where it took place in long stone sheds, now converted to cottages. More usually, mechanisation took woollen manufacture out of domestic production and, from the end of the 18th century, into the factory system.

Factory machinery relied on water power, and several early corn mill sites were taken over as woollen mills. In the north-western Peak alone they included Gnathole Mill at Charlesworth, renowned for the quality of its broad and narrow cloths thanks to the peaty water used in the washing processes; Diggle Mill was one of several in the Saddleworth area; Holme had three woollen mills, all now beneath Digley Reservoir; and Phoside Mill occupied an old corn mill site at Hayfield. Hayfield mills used to send large quantities of wool and cloth by packhorse train over the Pennines, via Woodhead and Holme Moss, to be dyed at Holmfirth.

Woollen mills were not widespread throughout the Peak, but there were a few success stories. By late Victorian times, fancy woollen shawl manufacturers Lowe & Scholes of Tansley boasted a global reputation, until shawls came to the end of their fashionable life. Over the past century, many items of woollen clothing have passed out of favour through competition from synthetic materials, yet we need look no further than the famous John Smedley knitwear factory at Lea Bridge to see that British woollens continue to enjoy a world wide reputation ... and flocks of sheep are still inseparable from the landscape of the Peak.

SOURCES

ADAM, William (1843) *Gem of the Peak*. Longman.

ANON. (1893) *The Matlocks and Bakewell*. Republished by the Arkwright Society 1984.

BERESFORD, William (1864-5) Notes on a Portion of the Northern Borders of Staffordshire. *The Reliquary*, 5. Bemrose.

BRUSHFIELD, Thomas (1865-6) Reminiscences of Ashford-in-the-Water, Sixty Years Ago. *The Reliquary*, 6. Bemrose.

BUNTING, Julie (1990) Time Out of Mind: Two Dales. *The Peak Advertiser*, 9 November.

BUNTING, Julie (1991) Time Out of Mind: Rowsley. *The Peak Advertiser*, 17 June & 1 September.

BUNTING, Julie (1992) Time Out of Mind: Edale. *The Peak Advertiser*, 22 June & 6 July.

BUNTING, Julie (1995) Monastic Influence in the Peak. *The Peak Advertiser*, 3 July.

BUNTING, Julie (1997) Counting Sheep. *The Peak Advertiser*, 5 May.

BUNTING, Julie (1997) The Pickford Name. *The Peak Advertiser*, 30 June.

BUNTING, Julie (1998) Apprentices: Necessitous Boys & Girls. *The Peak Advertiser*, 23 November.

BUNTING, Julie (2000) To the Peaks of Fame: The Dakeynes. *The Peak Advertiser*, 17 July.

BUNTING, Julie (2002) Sheepwashes. *The Peak Advertiser*, 26 August.

BUNTING, Julie (2002) Drabbles Mill: A New Age Dawns. *The Peak Advertiser*, 9 September.

BUNTING, Julie (2002) China Stone & China Clay. *The Peak Advertiser*, 23 December.

BUNTING, Julie (2002) Wirksworth China. *The Peak Advertiser*, 23 December.

BUNTING, Julie (2004) Joseph Hayward. *The Peak Advertiser*, 20 September.

CHAPMAN, S.D. (1969) Cressbrook and Litton Mills: an alternative view. *Derbyshire Archaeological Journal*, 89. Derbyshire Archaeological Society.

COOPER, Brian (1991) *Transformation of a Valley*. Scarthin Books.

DANIEL, Clarence (c.1975) *A Peakland Portfolio*. Published by author.

DAWES, J.G. (2003) *A History of Crich*. Landmark Collector's Library.

DEVONSHIRE, The Duchess of (1990) *The Estate - A View from Chatsworth*. Macmillan.

DEVONSHIRE, The Duchess of (2002) *Chatsworth: The House*. Frances Lincoln.

EVANS, Seth (1912) *Bradwell Ancient & Modern*. Facsimile published by Country Books 2004.

FAREY, John (1811-1817) *General View of the Agriculture and Minerals of Derbyshire*. Macmillan.

FORD, Trevor D. (1958) Inlaid Ashford Marble. *Derbyshire Countryside*, August-September.

FORD, Trevor D. (1958) The Black Marble of Ashford-in-the-Water. *The Liverpool and Manchester Geological Journal* 2 (1). Liverpool Geological Society and Manchester Geological Association.

GAUKROGER, Susan and HOLLIDAY, Joyce (eds.) (1996) *Memories of the Moorland Farmer*. History Live.

GLOVER, Stephen (1829 to 1833) *History and Gazetteer of the County of Derby*. Henry Mozley, Derby.

HARLAND, John (1866-7) Early Exports of Derby Lead. *The Reliquary*, 7. Bemrose.

HARRIS, Helen (1971) *Archaeology of the Peak District*. David & Charles.

HENSTOCK, A. (1969) Cheese Manufacture and Marketing in Derbyshire and North Staffordshire, 1670-1870. *Derbyshire Archaeological Journal*,

89. Derbyshire Archaeological Society.

HOWLETT, England (1891) Burial in Woollen. *The Reliquary*, New Series 5. Bemrose.

JEWITT, Llewellyn (1865-6) The Traders' Tokens of Derbyshire. *The Reliquary*, 6. Bemrose.

KELLY'S *Directories of Derbyshire*, all volumes 1876-1936.

MACKENZIE, M.H. (1963) Calver Mill and its Owners. *Derbyshire Archaeological Journal*, 83. Derbyshire Archaeological Society.

MACKENZIE, M.H. (1968) Cressbrook and Litton Mills, 1779-1835. *Derbyshire Archaeological Journal*, 88. Derbyshire Archaeological Society.

MACKENZIE, M.H. (1970) Cressbrook Mill 1810-1835. *Derbyshire Archaeological Journal*, 90. Derbyshire Archaeological Society.

MACKENZIE, M.H. (1970) Cressbrook Mills: A Reply. *Derbyshire Archaeological Journal*, 90. Derbyshire Archaeological Society.

MARSHALL, Geoff (2000) Peak Millstones - A re-appraisal of the millstone industry in the Hathersage area with particular reference to the fifteenth and eighteenth centuries. In: *Peak District Journal of Natural History & Archaeology*, 2, 53-74. JONES Melvyn and ROTHERHAM Ian D. (eds.). Wildtrack Publishing.

MCGUIRE, S. et al. (2002) *Hathersage Images of the Past*. Historical Hathersage Millennium Project.

MEEKE, E.R. (1996) *White Watson, Bakewell's only Famous Man*. Published by author.

MELLOR, George (1998) *Walks with George*. Betty Gouldstone (ed.). Hollinsclough Methodist Publications.

MELLOR, Gertie (1994) *Gertie's Story*. Betty Gouldstone (ed.). Hollinsclough Methodist Publications.

MIDDLETON VILLAGE HISTORY GROUP (2001) *Our Middleton*. Middleton Village History Group.

MOXON, Stanley (1948) *Umbrella Frames 1848-1948*. Samuel Fox & Company Limited.

NAYLOR, Peter J. (2001) *Cromford - A History*. Watnay Publishing.

NICHOLL, Revd A.C.F. (1984) *St Luke's Church & Parish, Sheen*. Published by author.

NIXON, Frank (1969) *Industrial Archaeology of Derbyshire*. David & Charles.

PEAK DALE LOCAL HISTORY GROUP (1989) *More Than Just Dust*. Peak Dale Local History Group.

PEAK DISTRICT MINES HISTORICAL SOCIETY (1968) *Lead Mining in the Peak District*. Peak Park Planning Board.

PHIZAKERLEY, Gerald (ed.) (1999) *The Diaries of Maria Gyte of Sheldon: 1913-1920*. Scarthin Books.

PILKINGTON, James (1789) *A View of the present state of Derbyshire*. James Drewry, Derby.

PORTER, Lindsey (2004) *Ecton Copper Mines Under the Dukes of Devonshire 1760-1790*. Landmark Publishing Ltd.

RHODES, Ebenezer (1818-23) *Peak Scenery*. Longman.

ROBERTS, A. & LEACH, J. (1985) *The Coal Mines of Buxton*. Scarthin Books.

ROTHERHAM, Ian D. (1999) Peat cutters and their landscapes: fundamental change in a fragile environment. Peatland Ecology and Archaeology: management of a cultural landscape. *Landscape Archaeology and Ecology*, 4, 28-51. Wildtrack Publishing.

SISSONS, David (ed.) (2002) *The Best of the Sheffield Clarion Ramblers' Handbooks - 'Ward's Piece'*. Halsgrove.

THORNHILL, Robert (1958) *About a Derbyshire Village*. Derbyshire Archaeological Society.

TOMLINSON, T.D. (1980) *The Mills of Hathersage 1800-1902*. Published by author.

TOMLINSON, D. (1983) *The Ancient Village of Hathersage*. Hathersage Parochial Church Council.

TOMLINSON, TOM (1989) *Hathersage: Its People and Traditions*.

Nottinghamshire County Council.

TURBUTT, Gladwyn (1999) *A History of Derbyshire, 1-3*. Merton Priory Press.

WAKEFIELD, Priscilla (c.1812) *A Family Tour Through the British Empire*. Darton.

WALKER, W. (1951) *A History of Tideswell*. Edmunds, Chesterfield.

WIGFULL, Phil (1997) The Dakeyne Mill & its Romping Lion. *Wind and Water Mills*, 16. Midland Wind and Water Mills Group.

WILLIES, L.; GREGORY, K.; & PARKER, H. (1989) *Millclose: The Mine that Drowned*. Scarthin Books.

WIGGLESWORTH, George (2001) *Leawood: An Industrial Hamlet*. Dethick, Lea & Holloway Historical Society.

YOULGREAVE WI (1931) *Some Account of Youlgreave, Middleton and Alport*. Youlgreave WI.

PERSONAL ACKNOWLEDGEMENTS

The author gratefully acknowledges information received from the following people at various times over the past 20 years:

Fred Bailey (Viaton), Tom Bates, Bert Boam, Frank Clay, Claude Fearns, Margaret Foley, Dr Trevor D Ford, Cyril Goodall, Keith Hayward, Rosemary Lockie, Sally Mosley, Peter Naylor, Joan Priestnall, Joe Rowarth, Amy Schofield, Linda Slack, Ken Smith, Liz Stoppard, Harry Swindell, Ian Thomas (National Stone Centre), Martha Tym, Ron Wood. Also the staff of the Local Studies Library, County Hall, Matlock.